# Preparing Your Heart for Passover

*A Guide for Spiritual Readiness*

Kerry M. Olitzky

The Jewish Publication Society
Philadelphia
2002 — 5762

i

The Jewish Publication Society
2100 Arch Street
Philadelphia, PA 19103
www.jewishpub.org

"How Does the Journey to Freedom Continue?" by Tamara Ruth Cohen, is reprinted with
permission of the author.

"The Journey Song" from Debbie Friedman at Carnegie Hall, © 1995 Deborah Lynn
Friedman, music by Debbie Friedman, lyrics by Debbie Friedman and Tamara Ruth Cohen,
and published by Sounds Write Productions, Inc., is printed with permission of the publisher.

Design and composition by Sasgen Graphic Design
Manufactured in the United States

01 02 03 04 05 06 07 08 09 10 10 9 8 7 6 5 4 3 2 1

Library of Congress Cataloging-in-Publication Data

Olitzky, Kerry M.
    Preparing your heart for Passover : a guide for spititual readiness / Kerry M. Olitzky,
        p. cm.
    ISNBN 0-8276-0705-9
    1. Passover. I. Title

 BM696.P3 O48 2002
 296.4'37--dc21                                                        2001038960

*For Howard and Diane Zack*

# Table of Contents

# Acknowledgments

This book began as an idea several years ago as I was preparing for Passover in my own home. And each Passover since that time, as I reviewed the process of my own preparation and the progress that I made each year, I knew that such a book had to be written. But it took some time to develop a model that was applicable to the variety of ways Jews prepare for the holiday, regardless of their denominational affiliation. Thus, this book may be called transdenominational or even post-denominational, for I believe it is the process of taking Judaism seriously that separates one group of Jews from one another. Additionally, I believe that standards in Judaism should not describe what we do but should instead provide us with goals toward which to aspire. So I wanted to provide individuals with an opportunity for a more meaningful seder through its preparation and participation: new standards toward which they might strive.

I must thank some people who helped me frame many of the ideas in this volume. I should begin by thanking Rabbi Rachel Sabath, who helped me realize that the dream of this book was possible—and even helped me get started on it. Though the words are mine, many of the ideas were inspired by our conversations and by our learning together about preparing for Pesah. My debt to her in this regard can be neither overstated nor repaid. I also want to thank Dr. Ellen Frankel, editor-in-chief of The Jewish Publication Society, who constantly stood by me and urged me to reach further and deeper. She understands that the journey of the soul begins in the desert. Other members of the staff at JPS have been equally helpful, particularly publishing director Carol Hupping and Sydelle Zove, former associate editor. The words and ideas in this book, although mine, have benefited from their caring and expert touch.

I also want to thank the many people who have sat around our seder table or have invited members of my family and me into their homes for Pesah.

This book is flush with the memories of their participation, even when such memories are not specifically articulated. They certainly color the background of Pesaḥ for me whenever I teach about it, study it with others, or celebrate our deliverance from Egypt.

I want to also thank my colleagues at the Jewish Outreach Institute in New York and the many people we serve, for whom the experience of Pesaḥ and the vision it inspires is a leitmotif for the work in which we are engaged.

Finally, I thank my family—my wife, Sheryl, and our sons, Avi and Jesse—who continue to inspire and guide me through each step that I take on this journey from Egypt to the Promised Land. ❧

RABBI KERRY ("SHIA") OLITZKY
PASSOVER 5761
NEW YORK, NEW YORK

# Sources

I have drawn on many sacred sources throughout this book, particularly *haggadot*, which represent the largest single category of Jewish publishing, even more than Bibles. In addition, I have used the Bible; rabbinic texts such as the Mishnah, Talmud, midrash, codes, and medieval, ethical, mystical, and legal works; Hasidic tales and teachings; and contemporary wisdom by such teachers as Rabbis Irving (Yitz) Greenberg and Zalman Schacter-Shalomi. Because this book is designed as an aid to meditation and reflection, I have chosen not to overly intrude with bibliographic references. By such omissions, I mean no disrespect; rather, I am following an ancient Jewish oral tradition of citing teaching "in the name of" the teacher. ✦

# Preface

### What Is Pesaḥ?

Passover—or Pesaḥ, as it is called in Hebrew*—encapsulates the formative experience of the Jewish people and then ritualizes it so that individuals may embrace it in their own personal way. It celebrates the deliverance of the Israelites from Egyptian slavery and their journey through the desert. As a result, Pesaḥ establishes a paradigm for our individual journeys, as well.

The story of Passover begins in the Book of Exodus (1:8–11), where we learn that "a new ruler arose in Egypt who did not know Joseph." In other words, the Torah text tells us that Pharaoh (probably a member of the Hyksos dynasty that came into power c. 1700–1600 B.C.E.) *chose* not to recall that Joseph—through careful planning—saved the Egyptian people from starving during a famine that threatened the survival of the entire Middle East. This new king presumably feared that the Israelite immigrants, though living in Egypt four hundred years, might grow too numerous and take over the kingdom even though there was nothing to indicate the likelihood of such happening. Thus the Israelites were enslaved (so that they might build the garrison cities of Pithom and Raamses), and their sons were drowned at birth—a sure way to prevent an uprising by future generations.

The Torah introduces us to Moses, a baby who is saved first by his mother and then by Pharaoh's daughter, who adopts and raises him as her son. Eventually, God instructs Moses to deliver the Israelites from Egyptian slavery and lead them through the desert to Canaan (where, along the way, God will reveal the Torah to them). It takes ten plagues to convince Pharaoh to free the people. The Israelites leave and miraculously make their way across the Red Sea while the Egyptian army pursues them. They then wander in the desert for forty years until they are ready to enter

---

*Throughout this book I use the names Passover and Pesaḥ interchangeably.

Canaan, without the guidance of Moses but under the leadership of Joshua.

As a result, the Torah instructs us to mark this miracle through an annual celebration of the deliverance of our ancestors. We do so by reenacting the events of the Exodus by means of the seder. We are also given other laws that govern the celebrations, such as the elimination of all leavening (Lev. 23:5–8; Deut. 16:1–8). These basic instructions were elaborated upon by the rabbis throughout the ages and interpreted through community custom as the Jewish people traveled throughout the world and throughout history before arriving at this place and time.

### When Is Pesaḥ?

How do we prepare for Passover? How do we begin the journey from bondage to freedom, from liberation to Redemption? And after all the preparation, where are we really? Song stylist Debbie Friedman asks the same question, "Where does the journey begin, where will we go?/ Years pass, the answers have changed as we keep moving along."[1] It's clear that the annual preparation for Passover is a stage in our spiritual journey, a stage that gets repeated and refined each year so that we might move just a little further ahead. In between, there are twelve months (thirteen in a Hebrew leap year) of human activity that threaten to throw us off course. So we have to repeat the journey just to make sure that we stay on course.

There are those who say that Passover comes early or late: it never seems to come on time. Maybe this is because we are never quite ready to return to the memory of slavery, even though it brings with it the promise of Redemption. And the complicated nature of the lunisolar Hebrew calendar means that Passover can begin in late March or even in the middle of April. Regardless of when it falls on the secular calendar (some people hope that it corresponds to other spring events like school vacations), Pesaḥ always begins on the fifteenth of the Hebrew month of Nisan. Why Nisan? One midrash offers the answer: Rabbi Akiva said, "God brought Israel out during a month when it was most suitable to go out. Not in the [summer] month of Tammuz because of the heat. Nor in [the winter month of] Tevet because of the cold. But in Nisan, when it is most suitable to set out on a journey, when the sun is not too oppressive nor the cold too severe. And should you say, 'Why not in Tishrei [the fall month of Rosh Hashanah and Yom Kippur, in September or early October]?' Because that month begins with the rainy season."[2]

### Pesaḥ and Spiritual Seeking

Why has Pesaḥ become a paradigm for spiritual forward movement? According to Rabbi Yitz Greenberg, innovative Orthodox rabbi and creative thinker, "The Exodus is the most influential historical event of all time because it happened not once: It reoccurs whenever people open up and enter the event again." Moreover, he said, "By the magic of shared values and shared story, the Exodus is not some ancient event, however influential. It is the ever-recurring redemption; it is the once and future redemption of humanity."[3] So it is that every year in this season of our freedom, says the Sefat Emet (the pen name of Ger Hasidic leader Yehudah Aryeh Leib Alter), every Jew is made a free person and is redeemed from all bondage, from all that binds us to our worldly vanities.[4] Passover has given us that freedom even when the countries in which we lived were unwilling to do so. And Passover has become the model for freedom for many communities in the western hemisphere.

My colleague Rabbi Rachel Sabath recalls that one night in New Hampshire, walking back from Friday night services on a crisp March evening that was also the first night of Passover, her six-year-old walking companion, Rebecca, known for her awe and wonderment of the sky, pointed out that the moon was full. It was a perfectly clear evening. Above the small New England town, the stars seemed extraordinarily brilliant. After Rebecca sang her special moon song, Rachel told her that the moon is always full on the first night of Passover. Why? So the Israelites could see their way to the Red Sea and escape to freedom.

A friend walking a few steps behind approached and said, "Why did you tell her that the moon is always full on the first night of Passover? She may remember and be upset next year when Passover falls on a different night and the moon isn't full." They talked a bit about the calendar, of how Passover always falls in the middle of Nisan (all new months are determined by a new moon) and that by the middle of the month, the moon would be full. We can't always promise that there will always be a perfect night to see the moon on Pesaḥ, but Passover, like the moon, can always be full.

## Preparing for Friends

The vast majority of North American Jews join together with family and friends to celebrate the Passover seder in one way or another. The kinds of preparation for these *sedarim* that people undertake can be plotted along a continuum. The practices are rather diverse. Some people are meticulous in their preparation. They not only rid their homes of all foodstuff that is riddled with *hametz* (leavening) but they also remove anything that even remotely has the possibility of working like yeast. Some spend weeks scrubbing every surface in the home. It is the Jewish spin on spring cleaning. Carpets are shampooed. Floors are cleaned. Ovens and refrigerators are washed clean. In many homes, countertops and other surfaces used for food preparation are covered. Cabinets that might store unopened *hametz* are taped shut. Some people put signs throughout the kitchen: WARNING: HAMETZ. DO NOT OPEN. Even drawers and clothes closets are attended to. Then out come the Passover dishes, pots, and pans.

The physical preparation for Passover is arduous. As extensive as it may appear, for many, this is all the preparation that is necessary. They are meticulous about keeping *hametz* out of their kitchen, out of their home. That is what is important. However, this physical activity is inadequate. It should parallel the spiritual cleansing and soulful preparation that must take place if we are really able to move *me-avdut le-herut,* from slavery to freedom. This may seem like an absurd notion for those who live in free countries. For them, the spiritual lesson is even more important. As winter gives way to spring and the world is renewed, we look to also renewing ourselves as individuals.

## Preparing the Self

The rabbis understood this idea of spiritual cleansing. They encouraged the physical preparation as a means of concretizing the preparation of the soul. Like they did with many rituals, the rabbis took a complicated idea and brought it into the world of the senses. Yet, the message might be overlooked in the zeal that people exhibit as they clean their homes and in the Passover food-buying frenzy takes place in Jewish communities throughout the world. In my home, we buy more food for Pesah than we do during the rest of the year. It is all part of the pre-Passover excitement.

As we prepare ourselves, there are other themes that emerge from

Passover preparation, such as gratitude and wonder. We are thankful to God for the many things that transcend the deliverance from Egypt: for the blessing of each breath we take, for daily sustenance, for guidance in facing everyday challenges. We marvel at the specific miracles wrought by God, things that the generation of the Exodus taught us to fully appreciate.

### Getting Ready for the Seder

The entry to the holiday is not preparation, however. It is the seder. Rabbi Moses Chaim Luzzato said that the fully righteous person will have the fortune to experience the light of the Messiah before the Redemption at the end of days. I see the seder as the embodiment of Luzzato's teaching. In the Talmud, there is a debate between two colleagues, Rav and Samuel, concerning what specifically is the essential transformation that one should undergo through the seder experience. Samuel teaches that its essence is political: seder participants should experience the move from slavery to freedom. Rav argues that the key experience is a spiritual transformation: to live through the contrast of the idolatry of our ancestors and the religious liberation of Exodus-Sinai that Jews celebrate. According to Rabbi Yitz Greenberg, these views are complementary.[5] In Judaism's view, slavery draws its legitimacy from idolatry; democracy is ultimately grounded in the God-given dignity of every human being. The God who created and loves us gives us freedom as our right and denies absolute authority to all human governments and systems. Absolutism focuses against the Jews, for it senses that Jewish testimony contradicts absolute claims. Thus, idolatry and totalitarian enslavement are alike—they deem absolute that which is relative. The Exodus challenges both.

For me, there is even more to the transformative nature of the seder than the powerful lesson that Rabbi Greenberg teaches. Each Jew possesses historical memory, a collection of the life experiences of the Jewish people to which is added one's own story. It is embedded in the religious psyche of each individual Jew. The seder experience helps us recall this historical memory, which for some people has receded to the far back of the mind, and bring it to the forefront of consciousness. The seder helps us reach back and remember. It is a real experience and a real memory. The seder is not designed merely to stimulate the senses. Rather, by speaking to the experience of the senses, the seder is designed to stimulate the memory of the actual experience of slavery and redemption.

## The Transcendent Nature of the Seder

But the seder is not merely a religious ritual, although that would be sufficient. The seder transcends even the power of historical memory. It helps us to understand more profoundly that our life has specific meaning and value. It teaches the value of freedom and the dignity that is to be accorded each human being. Rabbi Arthur Green teaches, "The root of evil is the enslavement and the degradation of the human spirit, the denial inherent in slavery, that each human being is the image of God. That principle is constant and unchanging; we are as committed to it now as we were on the day we left Egypt. But the many ways in which that evil force manifests itself, the human communities still crying out for liberation from bondage, the subtleties of enslavement even among those who think they are free, the new categories of evil and degradation we had failed to notice for so long—all these need to be rediscovered and worked out each year."[6]

Freedom can transcend the shackles of slavery. It is a mind-set that emerges in the context of a relationship with the Divine. In that relationship, one sees the self as an image of an instrument of God. Rabbi Abraham Isaac Kook wrote, "The difference between the free [person] and the slave is not merely one of social position. We can find an enlightened slave whose spirit is free, and, on the other hand, a free [person] with the mentality of a slave. Intrinsic freedom is that exalted spirit by which [individuals]—as well as the nation as a whole—[are] inspired to remain faithful to [their] inner essence, to the spiritual attribute of the Divine image within [them]; it is that attribute that enables [them] to feel that [their] life has purpose and value."[7]

According to the rabbis, we begin preparing for Passover thirty days prior to the festival because at that time every year God shows particular lovingkindness to Israel.[8] God sets out to free the souls of the Israelites, little by little, from the clutches of their impurity, represented by the leaven. Such cleaning cannot take place overnight. It takes time, especially after years of the grime of enslavement having been deeply embedded in the soul (just like a therapist cannot help a patient solve in one session the issues that have accumulated over many years). This cleansing of the souls takes place each night during those thirty days, according to Jewish tradition, with one-thirtieth of the impurity removed at a time.

Then, when the candles for the holiday are lit, even then we are not fully ready to make the transition on our own. We still need Divine help, just as we did in Egypt. We are reminded by Rabbi Richard Levy that "it is not we who light them. We shall strike the match but God will bring forth light."[9] According to Jewish law, the lighting of the holiday candles moves us from the daily to the sacred. By illumining the profane with Divine light, we create sacred time. Then we make *Kiddush* to consecrate that special time and to identify its sacredness. Although we thus mark the transition to a specific Pesaḥ time, it really begins much earlier. That's why we have to prepare for that transition.

### Other Seder Models

Recently, it has become common to find a variety of seders that anticipate the holiday, although they are not considered appropriate by traditional standards: we are supposed to abstain from eating matzah for a month in advance of the holiday so that the taste of unleavened bread will be fresh. More typically, these seders are designed for women (with the added Miriam's Cup, designed especially to capture the expressed role of women in the struggle for freedom) or are interfaith seders that celebrate community cooperation and foster interfaith relations. In addition, many synagogues hold community seders on the second night of the holiday.

### The Goal of This Book

The goal of this book is simple. Through it, I hope to help people reclaim the spiritual nature of the process of preparing for Pesaḥ by cleansing the soul. I believe that the soulful preparation for the holiday will enhance the celebration of the seder and the entire Passover holiday. Such spiritual preparation paves the path for bringing us closer to God; and in doing so, brings us closer to ourselves. As a result, our work together will help move us on life's spiritual journey, which extends beyond the days of Pesaḥ.

This is not a book about what most people do to prepare for Pesaḥ: cleaning, shopping, taking out the Passover dishes, buying new clothes, setting the table. While all of these activities are important to the process of preparing for the holiday, the personal preparation is far more significant and wide-reaching. Thus, this book may be seen as a companion volume to any book that tells you how to ready your home (especially your kitchen) for Passover. It is not intended to replace any of them.

This book will also guide you to and through the celebration of the Passover seder itself, particularly if you are given the honor of organizing and leading your family's or community's seder. That is why its chapter headings follow the outline of the seder. Moreover, it will serve as an orientation guide for a yearly recentering on the broader and more personal, spiritual meanings of Passover. As you search the corners of your homes for any remaining crumbs of *hametz* (leaven), this guide will also help you peer into the depths of your souls, looking for any remaining *hametz* (which may also be defined as a puffiness of self; see p. 3) that may remain. Whatever "crumbs" may be left over are those of unresolved feelings that we must purge in the cleansing waters or incinerate in the flames (in the ritual of *bi'ur hametz*). The key to this spiritual preparation may be found in the various elements of the seder themselves. Thus, each seder item will be used as a gateway for our preparation. Some people relate in different ways—perhaps because of their different memories—to different items: *Bubbe's* tablecloth, *Zeyde's* homemade wine and grated horseradish.

Some people may choose to save this book for reading on the Saturday afternoon just prior to Passover. This particular Shabbat is called *Shabbat ha-Gadol*, the Great Sabbath, presumably because it preceded our liberation from the slavery that is celebrated in the seder. Some scholars argue that this day was originally called *Shabbat Haggadah*, the Haggadah Sabbath, because many people use that time to review the haggadah in preparation for leading or participating in the seder. Eventually, the name *Shabbat Haggadah* evolved into *Shabbat ha-Gadol*.

The process of preparation can be both rational and simultaneously spiritual. Through the process of preparing for the seder, for example, we learn that "tasting spring" is a profound experience that extends beyond just eating parsley. Similarly, preparing for the spring includes more than merely searching our local grocery stores for the freshest parsley to be placed on the seder plate. Such symbols serve to remind us of the spiritual work we have yet to do and the blessings we can achieve if we can successfully move from the Egypt of our enslavement to the promise of liberation that is implicit in our journey through the desert.

The seder experience is also about the adult development of our faith. According to Rabbi Zalman Schacter-Shalomi, "The going out from Egypt is an experience that every child must successfully pass through. Just as Abraham was commanded to leave his country, his birthplace, and the home of his parents (Gen. 12:1), so must every child who is to become an adult. Every parent must be ready for this Exodus and balance the ability to let the child go with a continuing concern and love."[10] Thus, the seder helps us to move each year further and further into religious maturity and develop more fully as adults. ✦

# How to Use This Book

This book begins with a series of chapters on preparation and cleaning. These can be read at any time before the holiday. The central chapters that then follow are each divided into two sections. The first section is devoted to preparing for the seder. While these core chapters were designed to follow the prescribed order of the seder, you may find that a chapter or section of this book assigned to one part of the seder helps you to prepare for a different part of the seder. That's O.K. At a certain point, each aspect of preparation comes together as an undifferentiated whole. The second section, which I have called *"Davar Aḥer"* (another interpretation) takes the reader to an even deeper level of understanding that will be especially helpful to the one responsible for leading the seder. That person may even want to keep this volume alongside his or her haggadah of choice during the seder itself because the *Davar Aḥer* sections guide you through the ritual experience and enhance the seder by calling attention to its spiritual elements. The book concludes by connecting the Passover experience with the observance of Shavuot forty-nine days later and linking Redemption to Revelation.

This book can be placed alongside the many books that help you prepare your home for Passover. You can lay it on the nightstand by your bed and read one chapter a night during the weeks preceding Pesaḥ, since these weeks are considered to be special and integral to moving closer to the spirit of the holiday. You may want to review Chapter 1, Searching for the *Ḥametz* of the Soul, and Chapter 2, Ridding Ourselves of *Ḥametz*, before you participate in those pre-Passover activities. And remember to read Chapter 3, *Shulḥan Arukh:* Setting the Table, just before setting your own holiday table. Similarly, at the end of the holiday, prior to your indulging yourself with the *ḥametz* you may have been talking about all week long, reread the final chapter, Anticipating Revelation: Moving from Passover to Shavuot. This will help you begin the transition from Pesaḥ to Shavuot and guide you in counting the days between the two holidays.

This book can also accompany your favorite haggadah as you prepare for the seder since it transcends any specific framework for your observance, though its chapters are related to each of the symbols of the seder. May it guide you toward a greater closeness to the experience of Redemption and help you discover ways in which your soul can be renewed and redeemed.

After using the book for several years, you will most probably discover your own rhythm for preparing for Passover and the seder. Let the thrill of liberation guide your use of this book, as well. ❧

# Chapter One

## Searching for the Ḥametz of the Soul

Most people think that the majority of the effort of preparing for Pesaḥ is finished once the entire house has been thoroughly cleaned. All that is left is the cooking! However, even after everything is spotless, the real work of preparation for Pesaḥ is just beginning. The ḥametz that we must work arduously to seek out does not make its home in the corners of the pantry. Rather, the ḥametz I am speaking of lurks menacingly in the recesses of the soul. So we have to rout it out from there. This kind of cleaning requires more than detergent and dish rags. It requires that we focus our spiritual attention on the debris that has accumulated in the soul since the last Passover cleaning. With a feather, candle, and spoon, it is customary to peer into the corners of each room on the last day before Pesaḥ. Some people may choose to use more original or more modern objects, especially those created by the hand of contemporary ritual artists. Still, the search is only a symbolic one that marks the end of our intensive efforts at scrubbing, washing, and cleansing. In my house, Pesaḥ is the only time my wife and I can count on our teenage boys to help straighten up and thoroughly clean their rooms—and even then it takes some doing! The usual protests soon dissolve in the frenzy of preparation. Our sons know that this is the one time when cleaning their rooms is not about personal space and asserting their adolescent independence over parental authority. This also applies to any other space in the house that they have "homesteaded," like a large chunk of the basement, or the closet that once held their childhood toys and is now overflowing with "stuff" they have amassed over the years. So the deal is simple: we leave them alone most of the year and they do not oppose us this one time.

Then, as a family, we tackle other parts of the house. We move the refrigerator, get behind the stove, sweep the garage. The extra freezer in the garage is defrosted and thoroughly cleaned. Any outdated packages that were hid-

1

den in the back of the pantry get tossed away. Plenty of what remains goes
to the local community food pantry for the hungry and homeless. And who
knows what memories can be found in the scraps that have piled up over
the previous months in a kitchen drawer! The stories that emerge from what
we have found likewise help us renew the act of the Passover Redemption
as we take time to talk, reflect, reminisce, and teach our children of their
past—and our own. We search out any elusive crumbs that might have
evaded our thorough cleaning and inspection during the previous days of
preparation. Because we want to make sure that there is nothing left, we
scatter a few crumbs in the corners of some rooms just to bring a formal
conclusion to the process (hoping that our dog does not get to them before
we do). This part of the process of readying ourselves for Pesaḥ usually takes
only a few moments, since it is the culmination of days (and weeks) of
extensive cleaning. (According to Jewish law, four hours of total cleaning
should suffice. Obviously, the rabbis were never in any of our homes.) Once
we are finished with this ritual—relatively effortless compared with what we
have been doing the past weeks—we "deceive" ourselves into believing that
we are just about ready to celebrate Passover: the miraculous delivery of our
people from ancient Egyptian slavery to the freedom of the desert that set
them on their way to Sinai and the Promised Land. After all, we have moved
our regular dishes to the basement or closeted them away, cleared the cabinets of our ḥametzdik foods, and covered the countertops with plastic wrap
or aluminum foil. (Some people have countertop covers specifically made for
Passover.) And we have "sold off" whatever packaged food remained
unopened, undonated, or otherwise unaccounted for. (This "selling" is a legal
fiction developed by the rabbis to prevent financial hardship by allowing us
to give up ownership while retaining possession of the ḥametz that is still in
our house.) So what else is there to do? Some of the cooking is even done.

Passover time is also often the first time in months that we open the windows, having kept them tightly closed all winter to keep out the cold. The
windows stick. They need cleaning. But once open, the fresh spring breeze
blows its inspirational winds through the house. This too makes the search
for the real leaven just a little easier—and softens the painful memories once
we find it.

Ḥametz is leavening, specifically the yeast that makes dough rise. Some say it is the starter dough that our ancestors used. It was allowed to newly ferment each year so that new bread could be made from its new yeast. And each year, at a particular time in the spring, a new batch of starter dough had to be made.

The rabbis suggest that the leaven transcends the physical world. This leaven, this ḥametz, also symbolizes a puffiness of self, an inflated personality, an egocentricity that threatens to eclipse the essential personality of the individual. Ironically, it is what prevents the individual from rising spiritually and moving closer to holiness. Thus, what ḥametz effectively does in the material world is exactly what it precludes in the realm of the spirit. That's why it has to be removed. Rabbi Arthur Waskow calls this kind of ḥametz the "swollen sourness in our lives."

Some people say ḥametz is also a term for the yetzer ha-ra (our inclination toward evil), which is understood by the rabbis to be part of every individual's psychospiritual makeup. The yetzer ha-ra is part of a complex of natural drives and urges (for sex and food and the like) that is held in balance by its opposite, the yetzer ha-tov (inclination to do good). Just as the rabbis understood that ḥametz can be used to make bread rise, it also has the potential to overferment and spoil the bread; neither is the yetzer ha-ra totally evil nor the yetzer ha-tov fully without guile. As yeast has its purpose, the yetzer ha-ra has its function. But this drive to do evil requires balance in our lives, what the philosophers refer to as "the golden mean," something that will hold it in check from literally overwhelming the individual.

Ḥametz is also the baggage we carry from broken promises, failed relationships, and personal disappointments that weigh heavily on us. It is the refuse of daily living, the residual stuff that emerges from poor decisions, mistakes in judgment, and moral failure. What do we do with this kind of ḥametz? Can we hide or sell it? Can we clean or burn this type of "yeast"? Dr. Tamara Green helps us to frame the question when she asks, "Into what locked cabinet do I put all the pain and struggle that made the last previous year so difficult?"[1] The process of searching out and eventually ridding ourselves of physical ḥametz (which is addressed in the next chapter) helps us to find a way to spiritually cleanse the soul. According to the author of Avodat Yisrael, the search for ḥametz is conducted after the thorough cleaning to remind every individual of the obligation to rid oneself of the yetzer *ha-ra.* Just as one removes the leaven by the light of the candle, one should eliminate the evil that dwells within, searching the heart by the light of the soul, which is the "candle of God." Only with Divine light are we even able to see the *hametz* that is buried in our soul. And only through that same light are we able to incinerate it. Furthermore, who knows what else might be revealed in the light? We might even see the ones we love just a little differently in the special radiance of this phenomenal light!

⚬⚬⚬

There is a story told about Rabbi Joshua of Kutno, a nineteenth-century eastern European rabbi considered to be an expert on the laws of *hametz* and its removal. His wife had cleaned all the kitchen surfaces and poured boiling water over them as part of the requirements to kasher (make fit) the area for Pesaḥ. She took out every book in the library and opened it by the binding, fanning out the pages to release any crumbs of *hametz* that might have fallen into the book while someone was simultaneously reading and eating. Then, in her zealousness, she poured boiling water over the rabbi's favorite bench. Unsuspecting, the rabbi sat down on the hot, wet bench and exclaimed (probably among other things), "Why did you do that? There is no halakhic [legal] requirement for cleaning so extensively. The Shulḥan Arukh does not require you to clean a reading bench!" In an ironic tone, his wife indignantly replied, "Huh! If I were so lax as to operate by the rules of the Shulḥan Arukh, the entire house would remain *hametzdik.*"[2]

Preparations for Pesaḥ are governed by personal preference and family custom. Some people believe that this is the one time of the year when they cannot be lazy about their observance. They believe that the deliverance of their family from spiritual Egypt may depend on it. So each person has his or her own way of finding and ridding the self of its *hametz.* These individual ways become part of the family's traditions. In their retelling, some customs seem excessive, while others seem inadequate. A colleague of mine was so intent on cleaning his oven that he used a small blowtorch to make sure that he was able to completely destroy any trace of *hametz.* In his zeal, he melted the oven's internal thermostat and found himself without an oven on the day before Passover—and with twenty guests scheduled to join him the following day. My aunt changes her purse for Pesaḥ, as well as anything else that might have fallen prey to *hametz* during the year. As did the wife of

Rabbi Joshua of Kutno, some of my colleagues open up all the books they own and clean them, fearing that some crumbs may have fallen into the spines while they were reading and snacking at the same time. And recently a friend shared with me a recommended method for teenagers to clean their orthodontic braces before the holiday in order to make sure that no ḥametz still clings to the metal. All in an effort to find the ḥametz that threatens our well-being. In my house, we move all remaining unopened packages of ḥametz into one pantry. We tape the doors shut and place a big sign on it to make sure that no one mistakenly reaches for the contents. Then our dining room—which we are meticulous about keeping without clutter all year long—becomes the center of our Pesaḥ observance: dishes, food packages, and everything else reserved for Passover.

In a similar fashion, we each develop our own method for cleansing the soul and the self. Some study. Others meditate. Still others find the path to spiritual purity in the context of community. And in the midst of these endeavors, the essential ḥametz rises to the surface. Then we get ready to clean. Through the intensity of that cleansing our soul begins to sparkle once again—and in its reflection is where God can be found.

# Chapter Two

## Ridding Ourselves of Ḥametz

The desire to rid ourselves of *ḥametz* develops its own momentum during the weeks and days just prior to Passover. Some days we are consumed with cleaning. It reminds me of the "nesting period" my wife, Sheryl, experienced prior to the birth of each of our children—that uncontrollable urge to do everything around the house just hours before the onset of labor. During other times in our Passover preparation, we only offer a light touch of cleaning—a little straightening up here or there, or maybe a light dusting. On Shabbat, of course, we refrain from it entirely.

In many households, the momentum of Passover cleaning builds with increasing frenzy from year to year. Eventually, cleaning and preparing for Pesaḥ becomes a permanent part of family routine, and people schedule their spring calendars—even their vacations—around it. In our house, my wife and I limit our travels and even social engagements during that period. We know the work that has to be done—and it can't be left for others to do. While some of our friends hire cleaning services, in our family this is the one time where the cleaning that we may eschew during the rest of the year is embraced like an old friend. We refuse to let others do it for us. We have learned in our spiritual lives that we must do the hard work ourselves.

Like the heavy spring cleaning that it parallels, brushing out the crumbs from the soul takes time. The process is neither easy nor straightforward. Layers of accumulated grime sometimes leave a residue—even a stain—no matter how many times they have been scoured. Everyone recognizes that. One of the reasons Pesaḥ cleaning is so laborious is to ensure people understand that the spiritual parallel requires a similar amount of effort. Like washing windows, one wipes, steps back to check for smudges, and wipes again.

To rid oneself of *ḥametz*, one has to first acknowledge that the crumbs are there. We pray that Rabbi Richard Levy's words are correct: "This is the first transformation wrought for Pesaḥ: *ḥametz* has become like the dust of the earth. Soon matzah, beginning the seder as a symbol of affliction, will be transformed into freedom."[1]

Once the crumbs—the remnants of past deeds—are exposed, then we have to root them out. Seeing a few crumbs on the surface, we quickly realize that many more must be lurking beneath. So we ruthlessly go after them as well. Here's one way to do this: Reflect back on the months since the previous Pesaḥ. Dig deeply inside yourself. This will be particularly difficult for those who are not used to such deep introspection. So find a place to do your spiritual work that is pleasantly nurturing yet not distracting in its beauty. Isolate those occasions when you were led by an inflated ego. Make a mental list of these times or write them all down. Sometimes putting a written list in front of you helps you to examine such occurrences more clearly. And while one or two may be insignificant, the force of seeing such an accumulation in one place makes for a powerful impetus for change. Read the items on your list quietly to yourself. Identify those people who are related to each act. Then determine step-by-step what must be done to right the wrongs that you committed. Since we are preparing for Pesaḥ, take a few moments to write down the steps. Sometimes the activity alone is sufficient to break the cycle. Often, however, the process requires that you confront another and apologize—and then repair the damage you may have caused. For strength and support, read over the haggadah. Select one section, or even one verse, as a *kavanah*, a bit of sacred text, a mantra used to prepare one's heart and mind. Repeat it over and over until it flows from your lips and from your heart. Take one item at a time and stay with it until you have brought it to resolution before addressing the next hurtful act. It will take time. That's why we start preparing early.

It sometimes seems that no matter how much we clean, and even after we engage in the traditional ritual of burning the few crumbs that we have found (*bi'ur ḥametz*), we still find more *ḥametz*. That is the function of the fictitious "selling off" of the *ḥametz* through an "agent" (usually the local rabbi). Rather than simply including everything in the "sale," I recommend that people deliver part of the *ḥametz* to someone who is in need—perhaps a hungry street person—or to a food pantry. The process of giving to someone in need will help you get rid of the remaining *ḥametz* crumbs in your soul.

# Chapter Three

## *Shulḥan Arukh:* Setting the Table

The Passover seder is not just any dinner. So the table has to be set just right. Throughout the year, we make a special effort to adorn our Shabbat table. It serves as an altar—a gathering place around which we give thanks for God's blessings. Similarly, at Pesaḥ we create such an altar, but the seder table is not just any altar, it is the Holy of Holies, the holiest of all possible places, the innermost precinct of the ancient Temple in Jerusalem—usually associated with Yom Kippur. When we prepare the seder table and then transform it through our words and deeds, we sanctify it and ourselves.

In our house, the process of setting the table takes several days. Since so much has been in storage, things have to be cleaned—even though they were clean when they were put away a year ago. Tablecloths have to be pressed, and it takes a lot of time to get the china to sparkle and the silverware to shine. We have to make sure that there are a sufficient number of place settings for our guests. Invariably, something has broken between the previous year and the current one. Usually, no matter how many times we add to our set, no matter how many guests we invite, we often have one too few settings of matching tableware. We turn that into the setting of honor, replacing the mismatched pieces with a setting from the china I inherited from my grandparents. We invite the seder leader or a special guest to sit at that place.

It is important to always show our best to our guests. Doing so is one way that we can communicate the significance of the holiday and its celebration. When I served a large suburban congregation in West Hartford, Connecticut, my colleagues and I readied the building as if it were home. For weeks before the holiday, we made sure that everything in the synagogue shined and sparkled. And we did not leave the task to the maintenance staff. We wanted to communicate to everyone the importance of preparing for

Passover and to let each member know that Pesaḥ was on its way. So we rolled up our sleeves and pitched in.

In my own home, we like to acquire or make something special to add to the holiday table each year. Sometimes, it is something simple, like an additional reading for the haggadah. Other years it has been a new *Kiddush Cup* or Elijah's Cup that we purchased during a recent trip to Israel. When our children were young, it was frequently something that they made in school. Recently, we added a Miriam's Cup, which represents the role of women in the Passover experience. Our china closet is filled with such artifacts, each containing irreplaceable memories. By adding something new, we add a personal memory to the collective memory that the table setting represents.

We also have to figure out how many people we can squeeze around the table in our small dining room. Every year, we come up with a different method of placing the tables and chairs. As our family has grown, we have needed a larger table and more chairs. Most years the table stretches into the living room at one corner and into the kitchen at the other. It seems crazy, but each year we are able to accommodate the exact number of guests we have invited, even as the list has grown and it seems that there is no way we can add even one more person. Although this is an evening of leisure and comfort, no one minds being a little inconvenienced at the table. Inevitably, one of our boys comes home from school and asks, "Can I invite so-and-so home for seder?" Even as he asks, he knows the answer. Passover is a time when "all who are hungry may come and eat." All who hunger for spiritual warmth and a sense of belonging to a people are welcome at our table. May they always find it in our home—and in the home that they will eventually establish for themselves.

Then we make decisions as to which haggadah we will use from our collection of family and themed *haggadot*. Some years, we intentionally take an eclectic approach. By providing each person with a different haggadah, we are able to be get a better sense of the personal perspectives on the story of liberation that become part of our collective memory as a people—and as a family. At other times, we experiment. We prepare our own haggadah, or we add selected readings to a traditional one. And when a new haggadah appears in the bookstore, we usually will try that one as well. Just as everyone is welcome at the table, so is every idea. If Pesaḥ is the foundational festival for the Jewish people, as I believe it is, then its foundation should be as far reaching, as expansive, and as inclusive as possible—just as the Jewish community should be.

Some of our friends actually use the haggadah as a family scrapbook of sorts. After all, this is what a haggadah really is. They add all kinds of personal items to this loose-leaf haggadah as part of the documentation of their family's journey in the desert, from slavery to freedom. Children's pictures, report cards, poems, the remnants of a shredded mortgage document, newspaper clippings, journal entries: whatever speaks to them and represents the journey of their family.

In my home, we begin preparing the table by laying out my *bubbe's* tablecloth. It is our favorite. She embroidered it for Sheryl and me when we were married. By using it each year—even as it loses its luster, as the threads become a little bare, as the number of food and wine stains increase—it connects us with our past and paves a path for us on which to travel into the future. It represents as much of my family's travels to get to this place and time as does the story of the deliverance from Egypt. After all, *Bubbe's* Egypt—and that of most of my family—was czarist Russia. From there, too, we were redeemed.

The seder plate occupies the most important place on the table. We carefully select or prepare the items that will go on it. We choose the prettiest egg for roasting. We use just the right amount of salt to make our dipping water. And we make sure that there are flowers on the table—specifically to remind us of the relationship between spring and our liberation.

Sometimes, we place the seder plate on a coffee table in our family room and conduct part of the seder there. If we are supposed to be comfortable for the seder—a demonstration that we are freshly liberated from our slavery—then it is certainly more comfortable sitting on overstuffed chairs and sofas in a family room than on straight-back dining room chairs.

Since we are not going to rush to eat and we are going to "dine" for a long time, we want to make sure that we have prepared accordingly. It's not often that we have the liberty of talking Torah and eating with friends and neighbors until late into the night.

Setting the seder table is one of the most important parts of our preparation for the celebration of Pesaḥ. We treat the seder meal as if it were the last meal before our final Redemption. Just as our ancestors did not know when they were to be redeemed from Egypt, we cannot be sure how soon the Messiah will be ready to enter our lives. (That future Redemption is one of the things represented by Elijah's Cup.) And we always have to be prepared to invite him (or perhaps her) to our table. At Passover, around the seder table, we have this incredible sense that the messianic era is at hand. We feel that if our ancestors were delivered from their slavery, then we can be delivered from ours—no matter how big or small.

# Chapter Four

## Kaddesh: Making Ourselves Holy

**B**efore we can do anything we have to prepare. We have to get ready. The first formal step in the seder is called Kaddesh (holy). This preliminary step prepares us to be spiritually transformed through the seder experience. We ready ourselves to return to Egypt as slaves so that we might be redeemed.

### Preparation

While some of us are uncomfortable leading something whether or not we are prepared to do so, I can safely say that most people are more comfortable doing things if they *are* prepared. We prefer not to be surprised. It can be discomforting and downright scary to approach things cold, unprepared. Doing so is something that we were taught to avoid, and "Always be prepared" was the advice of our parents and teachers. These words, in one form or another, even became the motto of more than one organization. As we grew older, we were not always in a position to prepare equally for everything we did. Instead, we adopted a pattern of professional triage, determining what we needed to be fully prepared for and what we could do passably well with less preparation. One of my colleagues likes to call this intentional lack of preparation the "Zen approach," giving it a positive, more deliberate spin. Such an approach even has some positive spiritual power because it allows us to fully experience something without focusing so much on its performance and also affords us the opportunity to put our trust in the process and in ourselves. Still, without preparation, there is a greater likelihood that we might fail the undertaking, whatever it may be. Occasionally, without adequate preparation, we can even put our lives—and the lives of others—in danger.

We should simply trust ourselves, suggests another colleague. Too much preparation spoils the integrity of the individual experience. Some people prepare for events by centering themselves through meditation or prayer. While some say preparation usually enhances the experience, I would like to suggest that with regard to Passover, the preparation may even be more important than the event itself. It is the preparation that takes the most inner work. The event itself then follows naturally and becomes almost secondary.

How, then, do we prepare ourselves to become *kaddesh*—separate, distinct, even holy, as the Hebrew word implies? One way we do so is by establishing a pattern of separation for the purpose of consecrating our entire lives. It is this separation that puts us on the path toward holiness. Thus, separation and making something holy is not a singular event. Instead, it is an ongoing process that periodically culminates in a single event or a series of events before beginning anew. According to Jewish tradition, this is why we begin each day with prayer, in a dialogue with the Divine. Such "conversation" prepares us anew for each day and the lives we live. And after six days, we welcome Shabbat into our homes, separating the holiness of this time from the workday world. Each step we take presupposes a step of preparation beforehand, and so we note the ending of Shabbat by making *Havdalah*—blessing wine and spices, and lighting a special candle.

We accomplish this level of separation by loosening ourselves from the grip the secular world has on us and instead embracing the potential for holiness that is well within our reach. The secular world is seductive. Its enjoyment makes it difficult for us to make separation. Rabbi Naḥman of Bratzlav says, "When you are about to leave Egypt—any Egypt—do not stop and think to yourself 'How will I make a living out there?' . . . One who stops to 'make provisions on the way [as is recorded in the Torah]' will never get out of Egypt." For the Bratzlaver, as is the case for many spiritual teachers of Judaism, Egypt is as much a state of mind as it is a place in time. Egypt (in Hebrew, *Mitzrayim*, literally, "the narrow places") is the narrow place, the one that restricts the freedom for personal growth.

So there are preliminary steps that must be taken to become *kaddesh*. According to Rabbi Abraham Isaac Kook, the first chief rabbi of Israel— before it even became a modern state—we were liberated from Egyptian bondage in order to bring liberation to the entire world, but first we have to liberate ourselves. Thus, our journey toward holiness, and therefore our preparation, involves two actions. The first step moves us *away* from the past. The second step takes us *toward* the future. In the midst of this two-step action, at the moment that we would assume is the least clearly defined, we gain clarity. Only by moving toward the future do we understand what took place in the past. So take your first step by letting go of the things that burden you from this past year. Then take your second step toward the life you want to create for yourself. Consider what you are going to change, what you are going to do differently.

Joseph and his brothers, we are told in Genesis, did not understand this notion about moving toward the future in order to comprehend the past until they neared the conclusion of their biblical saga of rivalry and separation. Only after the climax of this biblical drama, when Joseph revealed himself to his brothers, did he realize that his brothers' evil act of throwing him in a pit and selling him to the Ishmaelites, who subsequently sold him to Potiphar in Egypt, was intended by God to end well. Once Joseph understood this, he was able to explain it to his brothers.

The more one rises in spirit, the more one can accept suffering with love and rise above both. This is why the Talmud teaches that "whatever Heaven does is for the best."[1] We may not fully realize nor appreciate this idea, but we would not have gotten to this place in our lives—or to the seder table—had we not taken the journey here. The path to holiness is not a straight line between two points. It is sometimes circuitous and often includes barriers that bar our way. But every step we take brings us further along the path.

### Davar Aḥer

Most people translate *kaddesh* as "to make holy"—as they do any and all Hebrew words and rituals related to it (*Kiddush, Kaddish, Kedushah*). However, the Hebrew root of these words reveals a meaning more closely related to the word "separate." We make holy by separating out something—or ourselves—for a special purpose. It is an experience of consecration. Only in the context of a religious experience, such as the seder, is wine (or grape juice) elevated. Wine is no longer simply a beverage. It is not a form of liquid refreshment that merely transforms eating into dining. Nor do we hold our *Kiddush* Cups the way we hold a glass for quenching our thirst or for toasting in celebration. It is the custom in many families—as it is in my own—to hold the bottom of the *Kiddush* Cup in the palm of our hand so that it opens like a flower in spring. It is a particularly fitting posture for Pesaḥ. And because of the mandate of *Kaddesh*, wine then becomes a vehicle that can help raise the secular context of an evening meal with family and friends into a religiously spiritual event. According to Rabbi Naftali Zvi Yehuda Berlin, wine gladdens the spirit. It lights up the face. With each succeeding promise of liberation, our ancestors' faces lit up with a greater glow of happiness. They anticipated the redemption that was to follow once they were able to fully separate themselves from Egypt. And this liberation from the Egypt of antiquity is tied to the Egypts that we continue to experience in the modern world, as well as the Egypts in our personal lives that we are working hard to liberate ourselves from. Such an effort takes place in successive stages, four according to the tradition. Berlin also believed that this would be the case when the ultimate Redemption of our people arrives in four successive stages.

At the same time, the act of *Kaddesh* moves us from secular time into Passover time. It moves us into the forty years of the desert journey, a time that is difficult to measure. Once we remove ourselves from the confines of marking time, we are unable to mark it. In our desert journey, it moves us from all of our enslavements and permits us to taste the sweetness of freedom. The challenge that we face is how to turn a taste of freedom into an entire meal. For it is the spiritual message of this Passover meal that will nourish us for a lifetime.

# Chapter Five

## Urehatz: Spiritual Cleansing

*Water brings us back to the Creation of the world. It returns us to the womb. It carries us across the Red Sea. It nourishes us in the desert. It even reminds us of the bitter stops along the way to the land of promise. And water is the symbol of ultimate Redemption, as well. Let it pour forth!*

### Preparation

Cleansing the body is such a familiar behavior, so much a part of our daily routine, that we generally do not even think much about it—until someone in the house uses up the hot water or your teenagers (or guests) have taken over the bathrooms. Moreover, our younger children may not always look forward to their nightly bath with eager anticipation; nor did we at their age. Other acts are conscious undertakings. Some of us have the rare opportunity to luxuriate in a bath of suds, a hot tub or sauna, or a long, hot shower at the end of a rough day at work or at home with the family. Many Jews observe the traditional practice of ritually washing following the recitation of *Modeh Ani,* a prayer of thanksgiving, upon waking in the morning. Similarly, we have learned to wash our hands before eating for the purpose of hygiene and to ritually do so before eating bread. We even immerse in a ritual bath, a *mikveh,* for a variety of prescribed reasons. Some men use the *mikveh* weekly as a way of preparing to greet the Sabbath bride. Orthodox and some Conservative, Reform, and Reconstructionist women use it regularly following menstruation (and on special occasions such as before marriage or after the birth of a child). In anticipation of any special occasion, we make an extra effort to cleanse the body, hoping that we might cleanse a bit of our soul at the same time. We do not use the *mikveh* to get clean. Instead, we use the *mikveh* as a means of helping us to stay clean. Cleansing, whether ritual or routine, helps frame our attitude before going about any activity.

Spiritual cleansing is a complicated kind of soulful hygiene that takes more than just soaking in a tub or scrubbing with the latest line of designer bath products. Generally, it involves neither soap nor water. Rather, we are washed with Divine light, radiated by the sacred texts we study and the loving acts of kindness we perform. We see this light, in particular, as it is reflected in the faces of those we love. It's ironic, therefore, that having made such extensive preparation for Passover and the seder, when we wash at the beginning of the evening, we do so without a blessing. When we recite the prescribed blessing for ritual washing—which we will do later in the seder—we often say it without being conscious of the words of blessing. Many of us go on automatic pilot, and the actions and words just follow. It is what I often rather flippantly call a "knee-jerk" blessing. Perhaps that is why this is the only time that we wash without a blessing—so that we therefore are particularly conscious of the blessing by its very absence.

There are a variety of explanations offered by the rabbis as to why we wash but do not say a blessing. Some say that we wash our hands because in ancient times it was a custom to do so before dipping things in any kind of liquid. Liquids were thought to pass on ritual impurity. Others say that we do so because the ancient priests washed before approaching the altar. Tonight, the table is transformed into a sacred altar. By not saying the blessing as we begin the seder, we are made more fully aware of it.

### Davar Aḥer

According to Jewish tradition, we ritually wash our hands before approaching a meal that specifically includes bread (or, in the case of Pesaḥ, matzah) and recite a blessing. What makes this particular ritual unique—especially at this time in the seder—is that we are not beginning a meal and no blessing is recited. Thus, it is a spiritual cleansing that Jewish tradition beckons us to perform and prepares us for through the experience of the seder. Most classic Ashkenazic *haggadot* suggest that only the head of the household should wash the hands. In some homes, he or she is assisted by family members and guests, much in the same way that the Levites would wash the hands and feet of the priest prior to his offering a sacrifice during biblical times. As is the practice in our family—and in many North American households (and as is suggested by Sephardic tradition), everyone washes hands, because everyone is to participate in the spiritual transformation of the seder. It is a powerful ritual when each takes a turn washing the hands of another. Then we can all more fully understand what it is to become a "realm of priests and a holy nation." Some Yemenite families say the blessing for washing here as well as later in the seder. But in this case alone perhaps, the water becomes a sacred vessel—even without the blessing. The water connects us to the experience as an ever-present element in the seder.

This ritual of cleansing begins the evening celebration by quickly answering the question, *Mah nishtannah ha-lailah ha-zeh?* ("What makes this night so different?"—better translated as an exclamation introducing the four questions that will eventually follow: "How different is this night!") This night is different in every detail, and this kind of washing is indeed unusual. It helps us ready ourselves for an engagement with the past that is so powerful it feels like the present, as is suggested in the core element of the seder: *Bi-'khol dor va-dor ḥayav adam lirot et atzmo ki-ilu hu yatza mi-mitzrayim* (In every generation it is mandatory for each individual to look upon the self as if personally delivered from Egypt). It is this primary memory experience that links Jewish people across time and space, for each collective experience of the Jewish people becomes our personal memory. It is part of the metaphysical reality that is embedded in the individual Jewish psyche. When we can wash ourselves clean of the debris that clutters our minds and our memories, then we can relive the experience of our people; we can return to the desert and begin the journey home once again.

# Chapter Six

## Karpas: The Renewal of Spring

*Observing the change from winter to spring affirms
our belief in the Weaver of this rich tapestry of colors
that explode in nature this time of year. Karpas is a
fragile bit of vegetation, used in the seder ritual, that
epitomizes the renewal implicit in spring—just a bit of
green in a world that often seems bleak.*

### Preparation

Even if you live in a North American region that does not enjoy a drastic
change of seasons, you can feel the renewal that is implicit in these shifts as
spring sheds its winter coat and bursts into a kaleidoscopic blossom of color.
Growing up in Florida, we still knew that spring promised changes—if only
the opportunity for its permanent residents to return to swimming at the
beach, something reserved for northern tourists during the winter months,
and to reclaim the local roads and restaurants. One reason the Jewish calendar marks the changes of time and seasons is that these changes *are* such
powerfully spiritual events; singling them out ensures that each of us feels
the rhythm of these transitions. These changes remind us of the power for
Creation contained in everything that lives. Similarly, each new bud and
bloom is an affirmation of the order in the universe: night is followed by day;
death is followed by rebirth; despair gives way to hope. This seasonal change
is captured by the sentiment of the Psalmist—the poet laureate of the Jewish
people, whose words reflected the innermost thoughts of the common
folk—who wrote, "Though weeping may tarry for the night, joy comes in
the morning" (Ps. 30:6). Throughout our nighttime wanderings—perhaps
one of the reasons we are so tied to the moon rather than the sun—our
people has come to anticipate this exquisite pattern of nature as it evolves

each year. We renew our optimism through seasonal change, however it is manifest. Our spiritual life depends on nature, which gives evidence of the existence of a nurturing God, in much the same way as our ancestors experienced God through the miracles of the Exodus and through personal deliverance.

It's true that sometimes nature is not what we would like to expect: tropical storms, blizzards, hurricanes, tornadoes. But it is these rare occurrences that help us understand our dependency on the more normal routines of weather. Were we to experience these acts of nature more frequently and with an irregular regularity, then we would be unable to believe that spring would follow winter or that day would follow night, losing all the optimism that such change brings with it. And it is this optimism that has fueled the dreams of the Jewish people throughout its history.

There is little that compares to waking up, renewed and refreshed, on a bright spring morning. The birds are chirping, the sun is shining, and our soul has been restored to us. It's amazing that we can lie down at night, exhausted, overwrought, stressed from our day's activities, and yearning for some measure of release—and while we are sleeping, God takes our soul and restores it to us the following morning in much the same shape as it was at our birth, perhaps even better. We are indeed reborn each day.

Pesah is the time of year when the symbols of our redemptive experience are all around us, allowing us to take special note of the orderly world in which we live, of the everyday miracles among which we often walk sightless, especially when we feel that things are out of control, that chaos dominates our lives and the world. Jewish tradition encourages us to say 100 blessings a day as we make our way through the world. There is much to appreciate as we follow our day's routine. Rabbi Neil Gillman names this appreciation of the everyday as "miracles among the mundane." He writes, "Mistrust the Big Bang. The world is filled with the presence of God, should we know where and how to look."[1]

When we eat *karpas* (yes, you *are* supposed to eat the parsley), it clears the palate entirely so the tastes of the seder that follow can be appreciated without the influence of anything else. This small plant, easily crushed in its natural environment, exudes hope and effervescent optimism. How do we then prepare for its use in the seder? It's simple. Walk slowly with eyes open to the world. Breathe deeply, and with each breath know that you share the air you breathe with others. Instead of rushing off to work, take a few extra minutes for a leisurely walk in the garden, through a park, or by a playground. The inherent optimism of spring is most apparent in the faces of young children at play or new animals that make their way into the world at this time of year.

According to Rabbi Abraham Isaac Kook, "The winter season arrests the forces of growth. But this cessation itself, with the advent of spring, results in a powerful explosion of confined forces. So, too, the impurity of idolatry obscures the brilliance of the world, conceals its beauty, and restrains the good coming to the world."[2]

### *Davar Aḥer*

It's strange that even in the midst of the carefully organized ritual of the seder, which we carry out according to a specific set of guidelines, it seems we can't resist playing with Jewish law just a bit. We so want to be in control. That's the way many of us were raised. So after washing our hands, we eat only a small amount of a green (spring) vegetable (usually parsley) in order to prevent the legal requirement of saying a concluding blessing as well. That we will leave to a period of time following the meal, about halfway through the seder. If we dig deeper into this idea, we see that this is not a foolhardy attempt at manipulating Jewish law. The seder makes a point of helping us understand that this focus on the letter of the law (where we would normally advocate at least an equal emphasis on its spiritual underpinning) reveals its unusual spirit. In fact, this balance between spirit and law is a salient feature of the haggadah. This approach to ritual forces us to move along, to continue the process of the seder, rather than bog us down, so we can find our way to the conclusion and the redemption that is ushered alongside—the ultimate goal of the seder experience. The rabbis were anxious to help us relive the experience as quickly as possible since they believed, as I do, that it is indispensable to the building of Jewish character and identity. Each ritual step we take mirrors our individual steps from slavery to freedom, from personal servitude to world Redemption, from Egypt to the promise of Israel. Rabbi Reuven P. Bulka teaches that "the first part of the haggadah is actually the reverse dynamic, of our present thoughts directed to the past, to our sojourn in Egypt, to the agony of servitude and ecstasy of Redemption. Thus, even though our manner of eating the vegetable suggests a royal presence, what we actually eat and how we eat it suggests the very reverse, poverty and servitude."[3] We go backward in order to go forward.

But *karpas* is not eaten alone. We dip the greens of spring, the concrete promise of our Redemption, in salted water. The salt water tempers our dreams with the reality of our experience: We want to be fully free, but we must remember that we were once slaves. The salt water is made from the tears of the ancient Israelites mixed with our own. Tamara Green put it this way: "I have felt that the salt water in which I dipped the sprigs of parsley was made from my tears. But salt is also a thing of value." Salt has permanence even as it dissolves. This mirrors our own experience. Even as our tears dry and we find the strength to leave our pain behind, they have permanence in our memories. We no longer weep, but the bowl of salt water overflows with the memory of our tears. And memory, rather than history, is the heart of the seder.

According to Rabbi Richard Levy, "For each sprig that breaks through the soil to turn green beneath the sun, there are so many that remain hidden in the darkness, in hostile lands, in the narrow places of homelessness and hunger. We rejoice that there are so many places where the world is green; we mourn all those places where it is not. And so we wash the greens in the salt water of all the tears that flow in those places, and in the salt water of the sea You split as a reminder that one day, tears shall only flow in joy."[4]

# Chapter Seven

## Yaḥatz: Finding What Is Lost; Mending What Is Broken

*The seder urges us to look for that broken part of self and reclaim it rather than further distancing ourselves from it. To emphasize this idea, once we find that broken part (the* afikoman), *we then consume it. We make it part of us to remind ourselves that we can be whole again.*

### Preparation

To break something, you must first grab hold of it. But first we must find it, especially if it is hidden from view. That's why the matzah is hidden on the table, covered up. The one item that is most associated with Passover, the item that one would expect to be on full view during the seder, is carefully concealed. And even when we finally do uncover it, we will hide it once again. This teaches us that the liberation it offers is fleeting. We also understand the power of discovery—how it leads to healing and renewed strength even when it is only a first step on our journey. We break the matzah in a manner symbolic of how the ancient Egyptian slave masters sought to break our people. The joined matzot represent the layers of our people (priest, Levite, and Israelite) and remind us that when we stood as one, we could not be broken as a people.

The commentator Abraham ibn Ezra once remarked that during his extensive travels, he was imprisoned for a short time in India. To sustain him minimally, his jailers fed him matzah. Apparently, they knew—as we well know—that matzah is difficult to digest. As a result, it stays in the digestive system much longer than does ordinary bread made with leaven. We feel deceptively full, even bloated. Because of that, prisoners (or, in the cases of the ancient Israelites, slaves) didn't have to be fed as frequently. The very substance that nourished us also represented our downtrodden state—and eventually became the symbol of our liberation from bondage.

Through the means of the observance of Passover and the seder, we took the very symbol that identified us as slaves and transformed it into a symbol of our freedom. Once we were able to fully understand its power, to wrest our fortitude from it, we were able to wield it to our benefit. We took our weakness and translated it into strength. We took hold of the matzah. What was once used in an effort to break us was made into something that could heal. And it continued to heal the generations that made their way through the desert. Our freedom now has profound meaning for us, because we remember that we were once slaves and that we, like our ancestors, have embarked on a desert journey.

Since matzah is the only thing that motivates this particular memory with such force, Jewish law demands we stay away from it (some people actually like to eat it when they are not required to do so) and not consume it for a month prior to Passover. By doing so, we prepare for its taste and the motivation of its memory through its absence in our lives.

### Davar Aḥer

Matzah is the central symbol of Passover. As the "bread of our affliction," it is what links us to the movement from slavery toward freedom. How strange that the first thing we do with matzah, the first really unique act of the seder, is to take a perfectly whole piece and break it! I prefer to use a whole large round piece of *shemurah* (guarded) *matzah*, which is made by hand with flour milled from carefully watched and processed wheat. Some people will use only this kind of matzah. Others use it to satisfy the ritual and then eat regular matzah throughout the meal and throughout the week. For me, *shemurah matzah*, prepared today just as it was by our ancestors, accentuates the ritual symbolism of unleavened bread.

We break what was perfectly whole and then hide it (as the *afikoman*). This moment is the spiritual introduction to the seder: What is broken and lost *can* be found. It *will* be found and made whole once again. This is the story of the Israelites—strong and then enslaved, broken and then redeemed—that has provided hope for Jews throughout history and offers personal inspiration for us today as well. We begin our lives as whole selves.

As we move through childhood into adulthood, some parts of us get broken, some parts of the personality go astray. We ritualize this process of becoming whole concretely through the mending of the imperfect and broken that takes place. Only when what is broken is reunited with what makes it whole, can the journey be complete. Only when we embrace the broken part of ourselves and claim it as our own—rather than pushing it away—can we be fully ourselves once again. Only when all are free, only when all are fed and taken care of, only when we can fully be ourselves, can Redemption and a completeness of Creation occur—what is often referred to as *tikkun olam,* the repair of the world.

In most *haggadot,* the leader recites a blessing during the ritual breaking of the matzah. According to a Tunisian Jewish custom, the head of the household takes a partially baked sheet of matzah and breaks off a piece in the shape of the Hebrew letter *vav;* this piece is to become the *afikoman.* We return the remaining sheet to the oven to finish baking. The leader recites: "In this way, God tore the sea into twelve pieces and the Israelites passed the sea on dry soil." We wrap the *afikoman* in a silk napkin. A seder participant places it on one shoulder and walks, carrying the burden of our history on his or her back, at least six feet with it, symbolically joining those ancestors who walked toward freedom. While walking, the one who carries the burden says: "This is in remembrance of our ancestors who left Egypt with their provisions bundled in their clothes on their backs." Hence, even before reaching the *Maggid* section of the seder, when the complete "telling" of the story takes place, we are already enacting the core notion of the seder: seeing ourselves delivered from Egypt, actually there at the moment of Redemption. We must all take the journey with matzah on our backs.

*Yaḥatz* (breaking and hiding) is what prepares us for the next step in our own journey. We will then be ready to more fully understand the story of the Exodus—retold in the *Maggid* section of the seder, when our personal narrative is fused with our people. Embracing the brokenness of the past helps us to pave the path that will lead us to the Redemption of the future.

# Chapter Eight

## *Maggid:* Telling the Story; Telling Our Stories

*The real experience of learning is directly connected to figuring out the right questions to ask. We can easily get information from others, but real learning comes with greater difficulty, for we have to study on our own. Good questions pave the path to real knowledge.*

### Preparation

When children come home from school, parents often ask what they learned. It is a scene familiar to many. Invariably, children will respond to this kind of innocuous question with an equally disengaging "Nothing." And that puts an end to the conversation. Parents feel estranged, and children feel that their parents don't understand what it is like to go to school these days. Taking a cue from my own *bubbe* and *zeyde*, I like to ask my children something that I learned from my grandparents. Instead of welcoming my children home with "What did you do today?" I inquire, "Did you ask a good question today?" This seems to me to be a better indicator of learning and understanding. When you know enough to ask a pertinent question, then you have reached a significant level of knowledge. We believe—and this is something the seder has taught all of Judaism—that the questions, and how you prepare to ask them, are often more important than are the answers. Most answers of meaning—rather than "just the facts"—have to be discerned bit by bit. They often have to unfold as we grow.

Such is the case with what has come to be known as the Four Questions (what my grandparents called the *Fir Kashes* in Yiddish). These are four specific questions that were shaped by the rabbis out of many other queries and that serve to initiate the seder conversation. There are plenty of other questions that need to be asked to satisfy us; these will emerge directly from the seder experience—at least, they do in our home. So what questions are on *your* mind? Begin by thinking about the weeks of preparation that precede the seder. What has been troubling you? Perhaps you want to know the role of women during the Exodus. Maybe you wonder why the firstborn Egyptians had to die in order for us to live. Couldn't God have forced Pharaoh's hand rather than "hardening his heart," as the Torah tells us? Write one question down at the beginning of each day while you are preparing so that you can think about it throughout the day. Then you will able to discover the answers during the seder experience.

Questions also help prompt memory. They help us learn how to probe the depth of our experiences and force us to reflect on them. When considering the trajectory of a lifetime of encounters with life, this Yiddish saying expresses it best: "To the unlearned, old age is winter. To the learned, it is harvest time." In sharing our experience with others, we relearn the lesson that we are attempting to teach and we grow as a result. According to the Sefat Emet, the Exodus from Egypt never ends. "In the act of telling about the Exodus [during the seder], the miracle [of deliverance] itself is continually fulfilled and enhanced."[1] When we tell the story of the Exodus, we are not just reiterating the history of our people's travels. Rather, we are sharing in the miracle of its journey.

What we learned during our experience in Egypt and during the Exodus was unparalleled. A midrash tells us, "A humble maidservant saw more [of a vision of God] at the crossing of the sea than Ezekiel saw in his vision [of the chariot]." Some of us spend our spiritual lives trying to have that experience once again. But the original experience seems to elude us. As a result, our spiritual lives become spent. The seder helps us to realize that the memory of the experience is ours. We merely have to recall it, which we can do memory by memory through the seder.

We learned many lessons during the Exodus. We have many stories to tell from the lives of our people and from our own lives. But what do these stories teach us? According to Rabbi Yerucham of Mir, the haste of the departure from Egypt teaches us that we should make use of each fleeting opportunity. The Exodus helps us learn to grab hold of each opportunity when it presents itself. Pharaoh could have prevented the death of many, had he but listened the first time Moses requested permission for our people to leave Egypt.

Similarly, we should be in a hurry to develop a relationship with God. As the Torah teaches (Gen. 22:3), we get up early to fulfill mitzvot. The term *hashkamah minyan* (very early morning minyan) reflects this sentiment. The early morning hours, just as the sun begins to rise, is my favorite time to say my morning prayers—before the rest of the members of my family waken, before I am drawn into the routine of my family responsibilities. It is my time to be alone with God, to tell God my story—as I tell others throughout the day.

### Davar Aḥer

There are many questions that are on our minds. Tradition has offered us four to ignite the conversation. The questions are introduced with this observation: How different is this night from other nights! Then come the questions: Why do we eat all kinds of breads at other meals, but at this meal we only eat matzah? Why at other meals do we eat all kinds of vegetables, but at this meal we eat bitter vegetables? Why at other meals do we refrain from dipping our food in sauces, but at this meal we dip our food twice? Why do we have to sit up straight for other meals, but for this meal we are permitted to slouch? In my home, it does not take very much to fuel the dialogue. Even before we sit down at the table, the discussion begins. It actually starts as soon as we begin the very first activity of Passover preparation, even if that is something as simple as buying cleaning supplies. The rabbis never intended these Four Questions to become so quickly fixed in the haggadah. The Malbim, in his *Midrash Haggadah,* suggests that the rabbis required the Four Questions to be asked right before the *Maggid* section of the seder because they represent different categories of questions. Thus, they became the first in a long list that would be filled in by seder participants.

According to the Malbim, the first two questions (regarding matzah and *maror*) reflect the concepts of slavery and oppression, hardship and bitterness. The last two questions (concerning dipping food and reclining) correspond to the concepts of emancipation and liberty, Redemption and freedom. The Malbim puts it this way: "Through the sudden and startling contrast of these two antithetical states of being represented by the very items which are part of the evening's activity, we create within ourselves a sincere appreciation for the kindness God has done for us, and we increase our desire to thank God. When we face the fact that at one moment we were eating matzah and *maror,* living painful and frustrated lives as slaves to a persecuting Pharaoh, and at the next moment our lives were turned around and we were dipping our food and reclining during our meals like noble aristocrats, our natural reaction should be to feel full of gratitude to God for God's magnificent magnanimity."[2]

We tell the story of the Exodus so that we can actually hear ourselves telling it, so that the words might help us to develop an ongoing posture for gratitude in our lives. We create memories for ourselves and for others. In doing so, we accomplish both.

# Chapter Nine

## *Ha Laḥma Anya:* This Is the Bread of Memory

*The statement* ha laḥma anya *(this is the bread of our affliction), written in Aramaic—unlike the majority of the haggadah, which is in Hebrew—becomes the formal introduction to the seder experience. This bread reminds us of our servitude even as it reminds us of our freedom. As we taste it, we are brought back to Egypt, poised for the promise of Redemption.*

### Preparation

First things first. You can't have a seder without matzah. And it wouldn't be a seder without telling the story—in one way or another—of how matzah began and of how it developed a necessary relationship with Passover. While there are many explanations, the one you call your own is the most important. Only then can you connect your acts of preparation with the story of the Exodus. As you take the matzah off the shelf at your local grocery store, you might even be surprised by the seasonally exorbitant price. Say to yourself or to your children or anyone else with you: "This is the bread of affliction that our ancestors ate in Egypt." (Don't think that this statement is reserved for a particular seder moment alone.) Do the same thing when you return home and put the package away, and when you eventually put out the matzah for the seder itself. Extend the ritual of the seder into its days or weeks of preparation. Pause for a moment and imagine the Israelites—not in a supermarket or kosher grocery store buying colorful, sealed boxes. Instead, close your eyes and see our ancestors in the desert, hastily preparing for an unknown journey, mixing flour and water, baking it as they ran for freedom under the glare of the hot Middle Eastern sun. The flour and water mixture is everywhere. It seeps into the crevices of tired and over-worked hands, under the fingernails, even in one's hair. It must have been a messy scene as thousands prepared bread that would not rise for the journey. Conjure up the memory of your own family participating in the preparation and baking of the matzah many generations ago.

Some people like to visit a matzah factory. These small assembly lines are often set up temporarily for a period of time prior to Pesaḥ and become sacred precincts of sorts, like the temporary dwellings in the desert. Don't forget that this is one bakery where you are unlikely to get to taste the products because, according to most rabbis, one should eat no matzah until the *Motzi Matzah* section of the seder. (And, as we have learned, no matzah is permitted for at least thirty days prior to Pesaḥ so that the taste may be "fresh"—perhaps a poor choice of terms—in your mouth.) Most probably, our ancestors did not have permanent dwellings as slaves. They assembled tent cities wherever they were forced to work. For many, the connection to the actual baking of matzah prior to the seder raises the matzah beyond its literal meaning. According to the logic of spirituality, by taking on this literalness, the eating of matzah transcends the rational.

When my colleague Rabbi Rachel Sabath was a young girl, she remembers thinking (after the leader begins the seder by holding up the matzah and declaring "This is the poor person's bread"—another way of interpreting the phrase—"that our ancestors ate in the land of Egypt") that no wonder the flat bread tasted so stale if it was that old! But that is exactly the point.

### Davar Aḥer

Actually tasting this "bread of our affliction" causes us to remember it. It helps us to "taste" the rest of the slavery experience: the dripping sweat, the dryness in our mouths, the smell of our bodies. In doing so, matzah is transformed into a "bread of memory." In the context of our celebration, morsels of flour become a foundation for our faith. The sensation of taste is a powerful tool that is overlooked in most spiritual circles. Many of us think that getting together with friends and family is mostly just about socializing and eating. Yet, the sense of taste often dominates Jewish ritual or is at least directly related to it, particularly during the seder. Perhaps it is because the sense of taste lingers for a long time even after we have finished eating. The symbolic tastes of the seder are mixed together to give us a "sensational" and fully flavored Passover experience.

The memories of slavery lingered for years after we gained our freedom. That's one of the reasons that we wandered so long in the desert. We could have taken a direct route from Egypt to Canaan, but we were not ready to do so. (Perhaps it is because the men who led us refused to ask directions!) It took the purity of the desert to clear our spirits of the lingering taste of servitude that accumulated over the years. We encounter the same challenge in our adult lives. It takes time to make changes after we have been doing something a certain way for so long. This is especially true of the baggage we carried out of our childhood or our young adult life. We can't expect to make such drastic changes so rapidly. We may have left Egypt quickly, unexpectedly, in the middle of the night. But it took time to emerge from the experience of Egypt. Eventually, just as the matzah dissolves in our mouths, so does the paralysis of slavery—even as its distant memory remains.

# Chapter Ten

## "Avadim Hayinu": We Were Slaves; Now We Are Free

*Our spiritual selves are identified by the core elements of our religious lives, that which makes us Jews and separates us from other people. What we are not willing to give up helps us remain who and what we always were.*

### Preparation

Is this notion of "We were slaves and now we are free" merely a descriptive element of the seder experience? Does it provide us with a framework within which we can work out our religious goals and aspirations? Perhaps it instead frames a primary element of preparation for the seder. For those of us who live in the United States, our freedom is guaranteed by the Constitution, the Bill of Rights, and the Supreme Court. The systems of government in many other countries have mechanisms that also protect the freedom of the individual in a variety of ways. If such is the case, how could the rabbis have made this claim for so many years—even before the notion of the modern free state? They could not have known where the journey of our people might take us. Or could they? Was the ultimate goal not woven from the outset into the fabric of our journey?

The rabbis were not just speaking about our physical selves when they spoke of freedom. They were also speaking about our spiritual selves. Even in years in which our bodies were locked in prisons, enslaved in foreign lands, our souls could fly free, but we had to be willing to let our spirits soar. When we saw the borders of Egypt as the whole of our world, when we saw Pharaoh as the only one powerful enough to offer us freedom, then we were indeed slaves. Similarly, even now that we are free citizens and can choose to do just about whatever we would like to do, we have to be willing to free ourselves from being locked up in a spiritual prison of the self. It is generally not others who keep us locked up. Instead, it is we who are our own jailers.

To find the road to spiritual freedom, we can take a cue from the slavery endured by our ancestors and the insights offered by midrash. In their commentary, the rabbis suggest, for example, that the ancient Israelites never took on the dress of the Egyptians. They never changed their food habits. The lesson here is that no matter where we go, no matter how far we have strayed into foreign culture, we are essentially Jews—and that intrinsic quality remains unchanged.

### Davar Aḥer

Like the entire Passover experience, the seder provides us with a concrete form for an abstract idea. The slavery of our people in Egypt was real; God delivered us from a specific place at a specific time. The spiritual slavery of our people was also real and God delivered us from it as well. It is one of the reasons why the journey through the desert took so long. Had the ancient Israelites merely been marching their physical selves into freedom, they could have made it to Canaan in a much shorter period of time. But they were simultaneously moving their spirits, and that is always a more difficult task, which takes a great deal more time. The Jewish people needed an entire generation to remove the shackles from the past, to shake off the servitude that had been learned in Egypt and to regain the sense of promise and optimism that only the road through the desert could offer.

For Jews, physical freedom and spiritual freedom are elements that cannot be separated from each other. Without both, we remain locked in servitude. Throughout much of our history, we worked to free the Jewish body—and even today we are still working to do so in certain parts of the world. In an ironic twist of history, now that our bodies are free, we must work just as hard to free the Jewish soul from its incarceration.

# Chapter Eleven

## The Four Children Within

*The haggadah speaks of four children—four sons, actually—whose questions instigate the narrative retelling of the Passover story. While the ideas may emerge from four separate people and represent four different perspectives, the personalities of these four children lie dormant in each of us, coming to the surface at different times, in different places, and in different contexts. The haggadah may speak of four different people, but we realize that we are all of them.*

### Preparation

Can you identify four people who are close to you who exhibit the characteristics of the four children in the seder? And when you are about to meet them individually or as a group, how do you prepare for such an encounter? Perhaps it is your one close friend who exhibits these different characteristics at different times. Whether we are speaking about the different attributes of one person or four people each representing a particular characteristic, our preparation for engaging them is probably the same. We can't relate to everyone in the same way. Nor do we relate to the same person the same way each time. To nurture a relationship, therefore, we have to be attentive and responsive listeners. But even good listening is not enough; we have to listen intensely so that we might respond accordingly—when in popular jargon we say, "I *hear* you."

Similarly, the Torah was given in different "voices" so that it could be heard by different people. One midrash teaches that the Torah was revealed in the seventy languages of the world so it could be fully understood. Another midrash suggests that God revealed the Torah in 400,000 voices so each Israelite could hear it according to his or her ability. Yet, some people remain capable of hearing only the "how to" of Judaism. They only want to "do" Judaism. Everything else seems to pale in comparison to Jewish behaviors. Others are interested only in the "why" of Judaism. It is the rational, the intellectual that speaks to them, and they may care little for ritual or ceremony. Still too many others don't even know what to ask of the Torah—and may choose to walk away from it disengaged and unconnected as a result.

As we prepare for Passover, we ready ourselves to listen to others. We ask God to open our hearts to others even as we ask the Holy One of Blessing to open our hearts to ourselves. Our ability to experience slavery, to make the journey through the desert, and to taste freedom in the Promised Land helps us listen as the experience of others is told to us.

### Davar Aḥer

It's easy to read about the four sons in the haggadah and not give them much thought. We all know people who exclude themselves (evil), who are preoccupied with doing things according to the accepted convention (wise), who are foolish and do stupid things (not intellectually sophisticated), or who are so uninformed that they can't engage in a conversation (unable to ask questions). Some of these people may even be members of our own families. Perhaps they are our brothers and sisters—or our parents. We try to be patient with them, although it is admittedly difficult at times. That's why the seder (and its preparation) is a lengthy process. Jewish tradition understands our human impatience and forces us to take the time to listen, to discuss, to respond thoughtfully and appropriately.

By identifying these four kinds of children in the haggadah, our rabbis are also identifying four salient characteristics in each human being—in each of us. There are times when we all feel excluded (or intentionally isolate ourselves); when we want to do things just right (and forget about why we wanted to do so in the first place); when we do or say things without thinking (even when we know better); or when we have no idea what someone else is talking about and don't want to appear uninformed or "look stupid" (so we refrain from asking any questions). This is not a description of different people. This is us, who we are at different times in our lives, maybe even at the same time. And it is because we are afraid of what others may think, or even afraid of what we think of ourselves, that any one of these aspects of self becomes the salient element of self. When we are not prepared to acknowledge and confront this idea, then we indeed run the risk of becoming "children within" once again. Why do we sometimes feel excluded from the journey? Why are we meticulous about Passover preparation but not about the rest of our spiritual lives? What is it about Pesah that we want to know even as we realize that we do not have enough knowledge to ask basic questions? Why do we sometimes ask absurd questions in order to avoid doing what we have just been critical of? Go ask the questions and then listen for the answers to emerge from inside of you.

# Chapter Twelve

## God's Promises

*God promised to take us out of Egypt and lead us to the land of Canaan, the land of promise. And that is exactly what God did. In return, we promised to follow the Divine instructions, what Jewish tradition names as mitzvot, as sacred obligations. We realize that perhaps we have not fully left Egyptian slavery, but we also recognize that we have not yet taken on the sacred tasks of mitzvot either.*

### Preparation

According to Jewish tradition, God made four promises to deliver us from Egypt. So the number four figures prominently in the seder, although the promises themselves are always identified with the four cups of wine. Some suggest that five promises can be discerned in the account of the Exodus. However, since four as an element is so prevalent throughout Jewish tradition, the last promise was separated out as a ritual item and transformed into the cup of Elijah. But it is this last promise, the one that is contained in the cup of Elijah, that validates the previous four. It is our faith that provides a firm foundation for our experience. It is the promise of ultimate Redemption that makes the deliverance from Egypt worthwhile. It is this sense of messianic optimism that has motivated our people's journey through every Egypt it has had to endure. And it is this element that permeates Jewish tradition and makes the number four so important throughout Jewish rite and ritual. These four promises have pervaded the Jewish experience so significantly that whenever we encounter a series of four, we are reminded of this particular grouping and we encounter the promise of Redemption once again.

Judaism is not a conditional religion: "If you do this, then I will do that" (although there are echoes of such dialogue by certain characters in the Torah). Nor is Judaism a religion whose posture is defined by indefinite gratitude or undeserving grace. Yet, the Covenant is a partnership, an ongoing agreement between God and the individual. God promised to take us out of slavery and guide us to the Promised Land. It was part of the agreement that was given form at Sinai. In turn, what are we prepared to promise the Divine? We are prepared to live a life reflective of that Covenant. This is our promise *four*fold!

### Davar Aher

The world is replete with evidence of the fulfillment of God's promises. "I will free you from the burden of [working as a slave for] the Egyptians" (Exod. 6:6). "I will deliver you from slavery" (Exod. 6:6). "I will rescue you with an outstretched arm and incredible decisions" (Exod. 6:6). "I will take you to be My people and I will be your God" (Exod. 6:7). Most dramatic is the rainbow, God's promise to us that there will be no more Divine destruction of the world (Gen. 9:13–17). One flood—however inadequate it was to wash the world perpetually clean—was enough! Now it is up to us—another of God's promises. As an acknowledgment of the four specific promises made by God to our ancestors (and recorded in the Torah), we are instructed to drink four glasses of wine. Perhaps it should have been water, to remind us of the crossing at the Red Sea. But wine admittedly softens the senses. And it affects each one of us a little differently. We have sorely learned, as did our ancestors, that the drinking of wine is not for everyone, even if you are of age. (Therefore many of us drink of grape juice instead.) But the rabbis encouraged the drinking of the wine nonetheless in order to emphasize to the individual that during the seder, we don't have to maintain all of our cognitive faculties. This may seem inconsistent with spirituality, but the rabbis urged the drinking of holiday wine in prescribed contexts as part of our holiday celebration. We can relax. We don't have to be constantly on our guard, as we once were forced to be. God is going to take care of us as we make our journey. For the seder, the promise is time-specific, but the rabbis want us to understand that they are talking about the journey of our lives. (Here the notion of a spiritual journey is important. Don't make the mistake of consuming the wine and then making a *real* journey on the road. Perhaps this concern is one of the reasons behind the traditional prohibition against driving on the Passover holiday.)

As you leave the seder, know that God will guide you on your journey in life. And that indeed is a promise!

# Chapter Thirteen

## Come and Learn: Experience Is Our Teacher

*We can only learn Judaism by doing it. And Judaism can only be embraced by fully engaging in its tradition and rituals. Then armed with this body of experiences, we can invite others to "come and learn."*

### Preparation

Some people think that Passover is a holiday that requires a lot of cognitive information before it can be celebrated "correctly." It is not coincidental that the words *experience* and *expertise* are related in origin. By experiencing Passover, you gain the requisite expertise. And some information will enhance the experience of the seder, though it can never replace it. You can't learn *about* Passover in the classroom or the library. You can only *learn* about Passover by sitting (or shall we say reclining) around the Passover table. So don't be in a hurry to eat the main course. And refrain from rushing through the story to finish the seder quickly. Savor the details as much as you savor the food. Be prepared to linger at the table late into the night. It was in the darkness of the night that we were able to see the light of freedom shining brightly and leading us on our way. Enjoy the company of your liberated family members, neighbors, and friends. Relish the fact that freedom has given you the means to eat in such luxury.

For some people, this notion of learning by sitting will not be enough. Like one of the four children mentioned in the haggadah, they want all of the specifics. They want to know why we do each and every aspect of the seder in a particular way. And as we talk about the physical aspects of the seder, we can probably provide them with most of the answers. The spiritual learning taking place at the seder cannot be found in books that provide facts and figures; such learning can only be found in the sacred texts of our lives. Once we learn how to "read" these books, then we can prepare for the seder. But here's the spiritual logic: The seder itself helps us to learn how to read the sacred texts of our lives. It takes the experience of slavery and freedom as we move through the concrete and the spiritual to gain insight and inspiration while moving us forward in our journey.

### Davar Aḥer

When I am engaged in the study of sacred text, preferably with a *ḥavruta* partner, a study-buddy, I often experience the presence of God. Perhaps it is because what we are studying is so related to God, or perhaps the act of studying opens my heart to the potential to experience the Divine. Or maybe the prophet Micah's question ("What does God require of us?") permeates my study and heightens the activity that must follow. With the haggadah, the sacred text comes alive. The story of our people literally jumps off the pages. As I think about the journey of the Israelites from Egypt to the Promised Land, I also think about my grandparents traveling from their Russian shtetl to these American shores, this *goldene medina* that they embraced because it gave them refuge from their own encounters with slavery.

Every seasoned educator knows that a straightforward lecture is usually the least desirable format for real learning. So the haggadah does not present itself as a standard narrative that might tempt the seder leader to use a formal didactic approach for educating the participants about the Exodus experience. The seder may not even be considered a monologue peppered with a bit of discussion here and there. Instead, the invitation to "come and learn" that permeates the seder and is the focus of this section is one that involves both the body and the mind and becomes a model for Jewish education through Jewish living. "Come and learn" is the primary posture for Jewish education. The seder teaches us that we cannot learn about Judaism solely in a classroom. But even that learning would be insufficient. By keeping the seder in the comfortable environment of the home, the rabbis are demonstrating that Judaism should not be restricted to the synagogue, either. We should learn wherever someone is willing to teach us.

# Chapter Fourteen

## The Plagues

As Pharaoh became obstinate in his refusal to grant Moses' request to allow the Israelites to leave Egypt, God "hardened Pharaoh's heart." God warned Moses not to expect Pharaoh to demonstrate a sudden change of heart. According to tradition, God anticipated Pharaoh's stubborness and used it to the Divine advantage; God sent ten plagues against the Egyptian people, each one more horrible than the previous one until as a result of the last one—the death of the firstborn—Pharaoh could not longer resist the people's desire to be free.

### Preparation

If the experience of moving from slavery to freedom transcends the specificity of the Exodus from Egypt, then the plagues have a similar universal hold on us. They are not just the frogs, hail, and blight that were unleashed on the unyielding Egyptians. They were also the darkness of depression and disillusionment that led us from one plague to another and surrounded us. Perhaps what was so frightening about the plagues was their relentless nature. The plagues kept coming and coming. Some sources record the plagues as having been unleashed simultaneously. That is what made them so overwhelming to the Egyptians. Only one thing protected the Israelites: God.

The same Divine force that sent the plagues against Egypt protected the Israelites. The same God that brought death also brought healing. This is the paradox of living. To prepare for any plague, one has to develop a relationship with God. That's why the Israelites did not fear the plagues. Even in the midst of total darkness, Divine light illuminated the path of the Israelites.

How does one prepare for the plagues? Through obvious means: prayer, study, and ritual. These lead us to and nurture our relationship with the Almighty. And if they don't, then we have to reconsider the integrity of our prayers, reevaluate the transformational nature of our rituals, and review the depth of our study. Begin and end each day with prayer. Let it emerge from the depth of your soul. Make sure that you study the sacred sources of our tradition. Enter into dialogue, for it is only through such dialogue that the teachings of Judaism become alive. (Start with the weekly Torah portion or with one of the daily psalms.) And use Jewish rituals to pave a path to God.

### Davar Aḥer

Each year, most of us take the plagues part of the ritual in stride. We may even assume a rather cavalier posture after a while, immune to the real human tragedy that emerges at this point in our story. Even the ritual of dripping wine on our plates to show the diminution of the joy of our deliverance seems to fall short of demonstrating a full understanding of the human dimension of the plagues.

Although the plagues represent a salient feature of the haggadah and we may even muse to ourselves with some self-satisfaction, "Look what our God did to the ancient Egyptians because they refused to 'let our people go,'" the plagues were harsh and cruel. They represent certain attributes of God that we prefer not to acknowledge. Imagine a world filled with darkness, so thick that even Divine light cannot penetrate it. Consider living in an environment that is overwhelmed by various kinds of vermin, things that threaten even the most basic routines of daily living. The plagues are there to remind us of the awesome power of the Almighty to effect change.

The plagues may seem to belong to a distant past. They may look like they should be restricted to ancient Near Eastern myth. But they continue to exist. They may not appear to be so specific or well rehearsed, but they endure nonetheless. And they continue to constantly threaten us, dressed in the garb of a variety of compulsive behaviors and addictions. The plagues the haggadah describes are primarily physical afflictions, those that attack the body. Contemporary plagues include afflictions of the spirit and are enemies of the soul. These are perhaps more insidious and threatening, for they destroy the inner self.

# Chapter Fifteen

## "Dayenu": When Is It Ever Enough?

*The song "Dayenu" teaches us to examine and express gratitude for all previous steps in the journeys that make up the little successes of our lives. When we assume a posture of gratitude, of thanksgiving, for each phase in our development, we can be even more grateful for our latest achievement or blessing. If we are not able to do so, nothing will ever be enough.*

### Preparation

When something good happens to us—expected or unexpected, when we feel particularly blessed—we tend to focus only on the good. Our latest good news becomes the only good news, often to the exclusion of anything else of merit that has ever happened to us. Sometimes the most recent experience, or perhaps the most dramatic one, overshadows all the events that lead up to it. We may even forget entirely the previous events that formed the foundation on which the most recent event depended. Had other things not happened, neither would this have been able to occur: the latest surge in the stock market; the latest business success; and, more importantly, the latest family *simḥah* or celebration. Those events in themselves might have been enough for us to feel blessed, to be grateful, and yet even more good happened to us!

Consider even our years of life. Some people bemoan each birthday, feeling the pangs of age creep up with each passing year. Yet, each milestone reminds us that we are alive, that we have made it to this point—when others may not have been so lucky. My wife, a passionate cancer survivor, celebrates each birthday—and each new gray hair and wrinkle—filled with gratitude and thanksgiving. Perhaps we should look at our lives as one continuous event, with birthdays simply marking periods of time along our journey, as a way of helping us to make sense out of what has gone before.

To achieve a posture of gratitude, we have to be willing to say "Dayenu"—even as we are working to reach higher ground. Thank you, God. Had You blessed me only in this way, it would have been enough. Had You led me through the desert on my journey only to this point in time, "Dayenu," it would have been enough. But You keep leading me—and I am continually grateful. So I will keep moving forward.

Take the time to make a list of the most recent successes or celebrations in your life. Next to each one, write down a related foundational event, without which the recent celebration would not have been possible. Start with modest ones and then add to your list those that are more significant and more meaningful. We might want to focus on a long list, but even this requires learning the lesson of "Dayenu." Ten stops on our journey in the desert are sufficient—though our mystical tradition suggests that the Israelites passed through fifty gates of impurity as they made their way in the desert. But ten reasons for thanksgiving, ten stops along the way, would have been sufficient.

What in your own life are you prepared to say "Dayenu" about?

### Davar Aḥer

Take the time at the seder, during the subsection of "Dayenu," to pause and reflect on the stages of your life's journey. Review each major episode, each transition. Then go back and look at the influence of minor episodes as well. How did you get to this place and time? Who was instrumental in making sure you got here? In addition to your parents, who were the teachers and mentors who helped you find your way in the desert? And when you inevitably got off the path prior to its conclusion, who set you straight?

Just when we think that the supportive and nurturing love of others is fully spent, more comes our way. It's the unique nature of the limitless supply of loving support. Love is perhaps among the few natural resources that has an infinite supply. As much as you receive, the source of love is not depleted. And to make things even better, it seems that the more love and support you give, the more you receive.

Taking this time to reflect will help you become spiritually present for the Exodus, the focus of the seder experience; for the experience of Torah Revelation at Sinai; and for the acceptance of Shabbat as a spiritual state that prepares us for our encounters with the everyday world. After all, these gifts came to us out of Divine love—not because we deserved them. And each time, when we thought that there was no additional means for God to express that love to us, more came our way.

When we experience a wonderful Pesah, we worry that the next one could never be as great, and yet each year we are able to reach even greater heights by reaching greater depths.

# Chapter Sixteen

## Pesaḥ: Making Sacrifices

*In the ancient world, the celebration of Passover evolved around the Pesaḥ sacrifice. This symbol has been used and transformed in a variety of ways, including the dabbing of lamb's blood on the doorpost to ward off the tenth plague. This idea has been replaced by the ritual affixing of the mezuzah, which carries the memory of Egypt with it, so that the recollection of slavery is never far from our homes and our hearts.*

### Preparation

The Torah is very specific about the sacrificial system, making it very difficult for many people to relate to. The memory of the Passover sacrifice provides us with a focal point on the seder table: the shank bone of the lamb (vegetarians usually use a red beet). As a symbol of God's deliverance, the blood of the sacrifice was placed on the doorposts of the Israelites to protect them from the last plague. While the mezuzah is primarily the concretization of the instruction to "place these words [of God] on the doorposts of your house and upon your gates" (Deut. 6:9), it is also a continuous reminder of Passover. Thus, every time we enter our home, we are reminded of Passover. Each time we enter our Jewish neighbor's house, we are reminded of Passover. Whenever we enter a Jewish space, we are transported back to the deliverance from Egypt. And when we enter, particularly for the first time, we may be motivated to touch the mezuzah; to kiss it with our fingertips; or to simply look at it, pause, and reflect on the Passover experience.

But there is more to sacrifices than acknowledging the sacredness of life by taking an animal's life for the sake of God. For we learn from that process—even now that the Temple system no longer exists—that in the context of significant relationships, we may be forced to make sacrifices. That is the primary function of the sacrificial system: to teach us that making sacrifices often transforms a simple act into a sacred one. How many times do we as parents forgo things so that our children may benefit! We do so in order to allow them to climb on our shoulders and reach higher. By doing so, each time, we prepare for Passover.

### Davar Aḥer

As moderns, it is difficult to relate to the graphic nature of the sacrificial system. Even the ancients used incense and the like to heighten the sensory experience (or perhaps to hide the smell). There is a small group of present-day Jews trying to recapture the primal nature of the sacrificial experience. And traditional Jewish theologians suggest that the Temple cult will be restored during the messianic era. While we may shy away from the thought of taking the life of animals as part of a religious rite, the entire sacrificial system looked more like a barbecue picnic than it did some primitive ritual of animal slaughter. Just as we enjoy our contemporary seder with family and friends, so too in biblical times we made our pilgrimage to Jerusalem with family during this time of year (and at Sukkot and Shavuot). We would engage the priest, vicariously invite him to join us in our family celebration by offering to him as God's representative the slaughtered meat intended for God. The priest would then burn off the fat and entrails, which no one ate anyway (and which made the best smoke and smell).

When Moses first asked Pharaoh to permit us to leave Egypt, it was merely to travel a distance of three days into the wilderness to celebrate an ancient sacrificial feast—then we would return to slavery. But with the Passover sacrifice, we do not return to slavery. Not then. Not now. Not anytime.

# Chapter Seventeen

## Bi-'khol Dor va-Dor: In Every Generation

*The lesson of the generations that is at the heart of the Passover celebration and at the core of the seder provides us with the foundation of the connection of Jews across space and time. Whatever our ancestors have done, wherever they have journeyed, we have been there too. And in those places where we have been forced to endure hardships, we have learned that God redeemed us then, as God will do so now.*

### Preparation

One of the central concerns of Passover is the telling the story of the Exodus from Egypt. That is what the haggadah is all about: the telling of the story of our people's journey from slavery to freedom. According to Jewish tradition, the telling of the story is so important that the individual who embellishes it is worthy of praise. Moses Maimonides, the great medieval philosopher and theologian, teaches that there are two levels of awareness associated with the Exodus. The Exodus was meant to raise Israel to the highest service to and understanding of God. However, if we have not yet reached such heights of understanding, then we should at least be aware of one simple religious truth: we were slaves and God freed us. I would add to that teaching: We are still slaves and God continues to free us. It is a continuous process.

Telling the story of our liberation can be accomplished in a variety of ways. That is one of the reasons why various seder customs have evolved over time in different communities. But what can we do to make sure that we see ourselves as *personally* delivered from Egypt, in accordance with this central Passover requirement? Is it enough to consider our daily deliverance from the Egypts that constantly threaten to enslave us? Or must we actually endure ancient Egypt, as well as revel in our Redemption from that narrow place? Will these words be enough? Will the sensory rituals of the seder be sufficient to remind us of the physical experience so that we can return there in our memories? What else must we do to prepare for our experience as slaves and our ultimate Redemption?

All we have to do is close our eyes and we can return there, to that very place where we were enslaved, to that very time when our freedom was taken away. We do not have to go very far: as we muster the courage to look closer, we will find that the time and place is not relegated to the distant past. Nor is it across the miles to a land that was not our home. Rather, the time and place is now: the attitudes that hamper us, the feelings of disillusionment and despair that hold us prisoner, the sense of hopelessness that threatens to tie us down. The seder comes to teach us this simple truth, as we are reminded at this point in our seder: God delivered us before and God will deliver us again—and again.

### Davar Aḥer

Sometimes you can be someplace and not feel that you are *really* there. Perhaps you are preoccupied. Maybe you have not let go of an event that happened hours, days, or even weeks before. It happens to all of us. I face one of the biggest struggles in my religious life each morning as part of my daily prayer routine. It's early in the morning. I need to rush off to my office. Yet I make sure that I take the time for my morning prayers. I know their benefit, and I work hard to prevent my plans for the day from creeping into my thoughts. As I pray, I try desperately to shut them out. And it is prayer itself that helps me to do so. It takes effort for me to be fully present in prayer, even though praying has become one of the most basic routines of my life.

Similarly, to experience the liberation of our ancestors, one has to be fully present at the seder. Leave the burdens you have been carrying back in Egypt: no need to carry them into the Promised Land. Sometimes all it takes is a meditation or reflection, a sliver of sacred text or a prayer, to help us become more fully present. Perhaps just a few deep, calming "cleansing breaths" that seem to emanate from the Source of breath itself will do the trick. For some, a change of clothing, a way of sitting (or, in this case, reclining), makes a big difference. Whatever it takes to help us get back (momentarily) to Egypt will ultimately be the ingredient that helps us leave it behind as well.

Our way of observing Passover may not be the way our grandparents celebrated the holiday, and it probably will not be the same way our children will do so as adults. But the obligation falls on us to remember our enslavement, to move beyond that painful memory, and to teach our children to do the same.

# Chapter Eighteen

## Rahtzah: More Cleansing

*Just as the priests washed before offering a sacrifice in the Temple, we wash so that we might approach the small altar of our table—and the relationships with those sitting around it—similarly, with clean hands and a pure heart.*

### Preparation

No matter how much we work to cleanse our souls, it always seems that there is more to be done. With life comes the accumulation of dirt and debris. We can't help it. It is part of the price we pay for living life at such a hectic pace. So during the seder we wash once again as a reminder for us to stop and regularly cleanse the soul. This time, we wash just before we are ready to eat, and we recite a blessing to emphasize the sacred nature of our task. Because we use the classic formulation for Jewish blessings, the words in the blessing for washing are indicative of the action that we are about to complete. This is true whether the act of washing is part of our normal routine of daily living or a prescribed ritual act. Even more so, like slaves we are brought to the table to eat, but still we can't. However, through the additional blessing that will follow, once we acknowledge God—and not Pharaoh—as our master Teacher, as the Source of life in the universe, as the Guide of humanity then we can continue the seder. We have indeed found our liberation in matzah.

While the recitation of blessings precedes the action in most cases, in the case of ritual washing, we offer the words of blessing *after* we have performed the act: "Praised are You Adonai our God, Sovereign of the Universe, who has made us holy with mitzvot and instructs us concerning the washing of the hands." It is a simple blessing that is only complete when we actually eat the bread (or, in this case, matzah). So the lively discussion that marks the seder is temporarily quieted to emphasize the relationship between the two ritual acts, *rahtzah* (washing) and *motzi matzah* (eating matzah). The silences between action and words, and then action again, wash over us like the water—and we imagine how quiet it must have been when the Israelites left Egypt in the middle of the night. However, the blessing remains truly incomplete until our souls are fully cleansed, just as the blessing of freedom remained incomplete until the Israelites reached the land that they were promised.

We begin the process of this additional ritual cleansing with our hands. We pour water over them rather than scrubbing them as we might normally do when they are full of dirt and grime. This emphasizes that while our feet might lead us close to or away from God, it is our hands that initiate action.

### Davar Aḥer

We ritually wash our hands before we eat—not because they are dirty, but because such washing helps us to more fully appreciate the Source of our sustenance, of both body and soul. We use water because it is the beginning of life. We use water *alone* because without it there can be no life. Just as we need water to survive, so do we need the food we are about to eat. Even though matzah is the food of slaves, it is also the food of our spiritual sustenance. The pouring of water from a pitcher (to simulate a natural source) over our hands helps us to understand this relationship. The water comes from above. We use the word *netilah* in the blessing to describe the act of washing, but the Hebrew word really means "lifting" rather than "washing." As we wash our hands in a ritualistic manner by slowly and deliberately pouring water over them one at a time, and then do so again (and even a third time in many communities), we lift them up to God, elevating the soul. Some might even say that we place the soul in our newly cleansed hands, and raise it heavenward. (We purify the hands so that we are able to perform this act of lifting without tainting the soul in the process.) Rabbi Richard Levy teaches that "this blessing anticipates the time when God will recreate the freedom of Eden, when without the sweat of human toil, bread itself will spring directly from the earth."[1]

Generally, a "washing station" is set up near the seder table so that participants in the seder may perform this ritual. Some people use the kitchen sink (and a specially designated washing bowl). However, it is the tradition in some families to pass the washing pitcher (and a basin to catch the falling water, to emphasize its importance as a precious resource) from one to another so that one person may pour the water over the next one's hands. As a sign of respect, children may wash the hands of parents, the reversal of a role that usually takes place in most homes. By helping to wash another's hands, we admit that just as we participated in getting them dirty, we share in the responsibility of helping to keep them clean. As we help to dry our neighbor's hands, we make a pact that we will work together to prevent them from getting dirty once again.

# Chapter Nineteen

## Motzi: Sustaining Body and Soul

*Although the matzah that is attached to this blessing may not be the most palatable of breads, we are grateful to God for sustaining us by means of it. Thus, this blessing of* Motzi *captures an essentialist approach to daily living. We eat to sustain us and we are thankful for the Source of our food.*

### Preparation

Just as we often take food for granted—even when it is the coarse bread of slaves—we similarly pay little regard to its Source. We open up the refrigerator, stop by a restaurant, sit at the table with food having been routinely prepared by others; we rush through our day with a muffin or sandwich in hand while we are doing other things. For our ancestors, even for those who survived World War II in Europe or the Great Depression in the United States, perhaps it was too hard when hungry to worry about the many things that those with full bellies can take time to reflect on and consider. But during the seder this is not your regular *motzi leḥem min ha-aretz* blessing (the daily prayer of thanksgiving for bread), for it is quickly followed by the blessing which acknowledges that sometimes bread comes in the form of matzah, the bread of affliction. Sometimes it is hard to eke out a living, hard to continue the daily routine, hard even to survive. In the silence that joins the two blessings together (for we never speak between saying the words of blessing and consummating the act), much can be heard.

This matzah bread is unlike the bread to which we are accustomed, particularly when compared with the beautiful braided tops of the Shabbat loaves that remind us of the Sabbath bride, or the New Year loaves that are wound around and around to suggest the circle of life surrounding us all.

56

Instead, this bread is flat and nondescript, unlike our people or its history. It was prepared for basic sustenance and no other purpose. It is nothing but flour and water; no culinary awards for this baked good. We hold the matzah close to our mouths, savoring every crumb that threatens to fall, so that we do not lose one small bit of its nourishment. That is what slavery does to a people.

This bread, this matzah, is also fragile. It breaks easily and unevenly, as might our people had they not been rescued. After four hundred years of slavery, our people got used to things in Egypt, even this bread of slaves. According to rabbinic tradition, God in fact chose that particular time in history to deliver the Israelites precisely because they had become accustomed to living as slaves and saw nothing in their future except servitude. They were born into slavery and there they would remain.

To make things worse, rather than sweetening the matzah bread with margarine or jam, we will later add horseradish to it—as we are directed to do—just to make sure that we realize how bad the situation really was for our ancestors. There was no redeeming value to our slavery, only the redemption that came after many years, at the hand of the Almighty. That's the irony. The desperateness of the situation led us to God, as it often does.

### *Davar Aḥer*

There are three matzot symbolically placed on the table—though there will be plenty more to eat for those who want to do so throughout the meal. Two of these matzot remain whole; the third, the center matzah, is broken into two pieces. Half of it has previously been hidden away (as the *afikoman;* see Chapter 7). With this first blessing (*Motzi*), we hold the two remaining whole matzot together, symbolizing the close relationship that exists between our slavery and our Redemption, which is only possible as our people stay together. It is ironic, but we could not have been redeemed had we not been enslaved. Had it not been for the experience of slavery, perhaps we might not have developed such a relationship with God. Traumatic events often bring us close to God in uncanny, unpredictable ways. It is clear that we could not have tasted the sweetness of freedom had we not been forced to endure slavery. Therefore we hold these matzot together to remind us of the wholeness in our lives that is only possible with freedom. We also recognize that we are not fully free unless we are working to free others. When we recite the second blessing (*al akhilat matzah*), we let go of our hold on the second matzah and instead grasp the remaining broken piece of the center matzah along with the top matzah. This action is perhaps our saving remnant. It emphasizes the broken experience of slavery.

Our people learned a great deal from being broken. We learned how to live as strangers in other lands. We learned how to treat the stranger and how to reach out to him or her. And we learned the value of settling a land that we could call home. As Rabbi Lawrence Hoffman likes to say, the experience provided us with this sacred sense of "landedness" that has identified our people throughout its wandering.[1]

After the blessings, we take a piece of the top matzah and a piece of the middle matzah, and eat them both while leaning (more like slouching, a familiar and favorite posture for many teens) on our left side—a posture of royalty that suggests carefree relaxation. This mix helps us to gain perspective on our experience as slaves—now that we are slaves no longer.

# Chapter Twenty

## *Matzah:* The Bread of Our Deliverance

*When people think of Passover, they usually think first of matzah, the unleavened crackerlike bread that leaves its crumbs throughout the house and slowly moves through our digestive systems each day during the Passover holiday. Matzah serves to remind us both of the experience of slavery and the euphoria of Redemption. As we eat it, we embrace the slave experience because without it we would not have fully appreciated our deliverance and the journey toward freedom.*

### Preparation

It is not enough to read about the experience of slavery or the values that our people tried to maintain while enduring servitude in Egypt. It is insufficient to talk about them or discuss them. At this point in the seder, the basic values of Judaism and the characteristics of the Jewish people are actually ingested. They are consumed so that they can become fully part of us. Every aspect of matzah—from the harvesting of the wheat, through its preparation and baking to its eating—is all meant to suggest meaning while invoking memory at the same time, something that the rabbis wanted to make sure that we did not miss during the seder experience.

Rabbi Ben Kamin calls matzah "hurry-up bread." It is born out of a specific social context that did not allow for leisurely dining. The ancient Israelites, like the homeless who people our city streets, could not afford the luxury of the enjoyment of eating. Instead, they held their slave bread close to them, fearful that it might be stolen. Their eyes darted from place to place, from person to person, fearful that their taskmasters might think they had taken too much time to eat or that someone might steal it (or their other meager possessions) while their attention was diverted. They were afraid for their lives and the lives of their children. And then suddenly, they were called to leave at midnight. Even a fitful night's sleep evaded them.

It is sometimes played as a children's game, sometimes offered as an educational exercise, but the question is rather profound: What would you bring if you were forced to leave in the middle of the night? Look around your home. What should be taken, and what can be left behind? What things represent the essential values that have driven your lives, the legacy you want to leave those who come after you, the things that are truly priceless and that cannot be replaced?

### Davar Aḥer

Finally, after waiting for so long, we are permitted to taste the matzah. Now that so much time has passed, especially for those who are impatient seder guests, we are permitted the luxury of actually *tasting* it. It reminds me of the times that I have returned to places of my childhood or even young adulthood and tried to relive the memory, doing familiar things, eating in familiar places, even trying to capture familiar smells. Things just aren't the same so many years later. And neither are we. After the Redemption from slavery, after wandering in the desert, we now *long* to taste the matzah. Quite a spiritual irony and twist of history! Now that we are free, we yearn for a taste of slavery once again.

Perhaps it is the same desire that the Israelites expressed throughout their desert wanderings to return to the place of *dis*comfort, the place of narrow places: Egypt. Perhaps we want to race back there to share the experience with our ancestors. Or perhaps we are often so much in a hurry to be bound by the shackles of modern-world slavery that we don't even realize that we are being enslaved in the process. We have deluded ourselves into believing that we are always in control, that we can change the direction of our lives, even in the midst of our compulsions and predilections.

Consider the incredible power of this roughly baked bread. A few grains of flour and water mixed together can transcend time and bring healing in the process; so say the mystics in the Zohar. Rabbi Naḥman taught that matzah itself is a sign of Heavenly conflict (noting that matzah is related to the Aramaic root for struggle). "Such conflict eventually leads to enhanced awareness and understanding of God and to greater harmony....The cause of illness, God forbid, is a lack of harmony. The four basic elements that make up the body are in conflict with one element rising up against another. Therefore, peace brings healing. This also explains why matzah is called the 'bread of the poor.' 'One is only poor when he or she has no awareness of God.'[1] This is the root of illness. Matzah—the awareness of God—is the remedy. This is why it is called the 'bread of the poor,' because it is the remedy for such 'poverty.'"[2]

To be fully healed, we have to go beyond the self. This matzah, because of its power to conjure up powerful memories, has an astonishing potential to stir us to action. This is a call for social justice, a call that extends beyond our borders. That's why matzah and the seder have become a universal symbol for many liberation movements, most notably the civil rights movement in the United States. This year, make sure that the last taste of matzah provides a lasting taste. Don't put your dishes away so quickly for another year at the end of the holiday. Leave them where people can stumble over them. Maybe that will move you and others to action.

# Chapter Twenty-One

## *Maror*: Bitter Memories

*In order to appreciate the sweetness and renewal of spring, which serves as a backdrop for our celebration of Passover and is intimately woven through it, we have to remind ourselves of our embittered experience as slaves. So we use each of our senses as an aid in bringing us back to that time. We force ourselves to eat bitter herbs like horseradish in sympathy with our ancestors who endured slavery. But because we know that Redemption followed slavery, we sweeten the* maror *just a bit.*

### Preparation

Some of us carry bitterness with us through life. Sometimes we are not even aware of it. Others revel in their own pain. They enjoy the role of victim and continue to perpetuate it to their own end. For many, this bitterness manifests itself in the form of anger, particularly as we recall certain memories. Few people talk about "family of origin" issues and mean our ancestors in ancient Egypt! It is difficult to recall what is painful. Often, we forget entirely—something our minds intentionally are designed to do to protect us—but preparing for the holiday helps us to recall certain things. When the issues that require our attention are out in front of us, then we can do the work on them that is necessary.

Memory does not always come easily. Sometimes we have to force ourselves to remember. When my son Jesse was about five, he broke his arm on the playground slide. He had just reached the bottom. Somehow the sand that surrounded the slide, which was there to protect children, refused to give way when his arm was thrust deep into it. Sheryl and I were in the park for his brother's baseball game. It was a beautiful spring afternoon. Then we heard the scream. One of the coaches on the opposing team was a paramedic. He immobilized the arm until Jesse could be transported to the hospital. Eventually, an ambulance arrived and we rode with Jesse to the hospital where—following x-rays and the like—an orthopedic resident set the arm and casted it without any anesthesia or pain medication, only some antibiotics to prevent infection and ice to keep down the swelling. That evening, as we were reviewing the events of the day, Jesse had absolutely no recollection of it—nor does he until this day, many years later. No memory of the ambulance or its sirens. No memory of the emergency room or the physician who noisily set his broken bone in place (a recurring sound I can still hear). No memory of the experience at all.

Painful memories have the potential to take control of our lives, even when we don't realize it. That is often when the anger emerges or, worse, compulsive behaviors and abuse of substance and people set in because the anger goes unrecognized and unabated. It is a crooked way of thinking, but we have convinced ourselves that we can sedate the pain through chemicals or behaviors—food to combat emptiness, sex as a substitute for love, alcohol as an antidote for fear.

Prepare for the bitterness by creating sweet memories of your own. It's one of the reasons why the rabbis instituted the seder in the first place.

### Davar Aher

One would think that *maror* is out of order in the seder. If *maror* represents the bitterness of slavery, it should come before the *pesah* (which was eaten on the night of the Exodus from Egypt itself). and the matzah (which resulted from a hasty departure from Egypt). But *maror* is last because contained within the bitterness of slavery came the potential for Redemption. It is a lesson many of us have learned in life. Out of our pain comes growth. Out of our bitterness comes the sweet taste of freedom. Some commentators even argue that we did not stay in Egypt as long as was intended. God redeemed us early from our slavery because the experience of slavery embittered our lives. Nonetheless, it was that bitterness which drove us to freedom.

Whenever I sit at the seder table, my mind is taken into the past, but not directly to the Israelites in Egypt. Instead, my attention is drawn first to the chairs placed around the table. I think of past guests who have sat in those chairs. Though the room is crowded, there are many who no longer join us for the seder. Who is not here with us this year? Who has moved away? Who has grown and started his or her own household? Who is no longer counted among the living? And whose chair can never be filled?

My memories of my grandfather are limited. He died when I was very young. My *zeyde* was a slave to the unfiltered cigarettes that eventually stole his life from us. I remember the smell of his sweat as he drew me close at the end of his workday collecting rags in Pittsburgh. But once a year, the memory of him changed, as he grated his own horseradish for use in our seder. This was one practice that he carried with him from Russia and refused to give up, even when his poor health demanded that he do so. And so with me on his knee, he would grate his horseradish until I started crying and his sweat mixed with my tears. From that experience, I learned for the first time the lesson I would relearn many times in my life: bitterness can be sweet.

Some people don't use horseradish at their seder. Instead, they use romaine lettuce because, like our experience in Egypt, its taste is initially sweet, but it later turns bitter. Some memories start out bitter and turn out sweet. It all depends on how we interpret them and what we learn from them.

# Chapter Twenty-Two

## Korekh: Adapting

*The historic dynamism of Judaism can best be seen in how our people have internalized the external culture of the host nations in which it found itself and how we processed it to make it our own. Music. Literature. Dress. Food. This is represented in the seder by what is called the Hillel sandwich, a combination of several ingredients that together make a statement about the journey. It has taken us to many places before we found our way home.*

### Preparation

This is some sandwich. Still, it's not the kind that I look forward to, knowing that it will stay with me for a while. The *korekh* sandwich is made of matzah (dry, crumbling, difficult to hold), horseradish (hot, biting, eye-watering), and a bit of *haroset* (a mortarlike mixture of nuts, fruit, and wine—its ingredients vary depending on family and community custom). And it has to sustain me until we are able to eat the main course. In my house, dinner is rather late—and it gets later each year. Truth be told, however, *this* is the main course, the main idea. This little sandwich represents the journey of our people throughout its history. In doing so, it is a contemporary reflection of our lives as well.

By bringing the bitter herbs together with the matzah, we come to understand how the *bitterness* of slavery gave shape to the *experience* of slavery. This is why Hillel the Elder taught us to eat them together. The mixing of the ingredients in this sandwich ensures our survival as a people in the face of our historical experiences. Matzah, *maror*, and *haroset* provide us with redemptive hope in the face of slavery. This is what helped us to survive in Egypt and elsewhere—and continues to do so even in lands of plenty.

The so-called Hillel sandwich has been assembled and eaten this way for a long time. With it comes the kind of family wisdom that is passed down through the generations via the sharing of recipes. Often that wisdom is shared in the hours before the seder, while parent and child (or grandparent and grandchild) prepare the *haroset,* a mixture that is supposed to remind us of the mortar used by the ancient Israelites to build the giant store cities of Pithom and Ramses for Pharaoh. So be creative with your *haroset.* Remember the wisdom you will add to its ingredients to carry its message into the next generation.

### Davar Aḥer

Technically, we are required to eat this sandwich, according to Hillel's direction and recipe, because we no longer eat of the sacrifice of the paschal lamb. It takes the place of the sacrifice, although we still retain its symbol on our seder plate. No additional blessing is required to eat this sandwich. The third or lowermost matzah is used, along with a bit of horseradish (my favorite is mixed with thick bits of red beets), and *haroset.* For *haroset,* we try a new recipe each year, along with the standard Ashkenazic recipe of nuts, apples, and wine. It keeps us connected with the Jewish people scattered throughout the nations of world. My favorite recipe for *haroset* includes dates. The combination of the mortar-like substance with Israeli dates (that connect me directly to the Land) is essential to the celebration of my Pesaḥ, for I cannot ingest the matzah of slavery, emphasized with the bitterness of *maror,* without the promise that the Land of Israel contains. And then, when I am ready, I recline to the left while eating this peculiar culinary creation.

But what did Hillel have in mind when he made the suggestion for this sandwich? Was he trying to encourage more questions? Was he perhaps interested in entertaining the children whose interest wanes at about this point in the seder? He was certainly not deluding himself or others into thinking that he was a gourmet chef. Perhaps he wanted to teach us about the complexity of the Jewish past and its lessons for the future. The Jewish people learned many of its values about interacting with others while in

Egypt. Its shared destiny was forged there. Slavery taught us to hope, to maintain optimism, and to have faith in Redemption, lessons we carried through history. God fulfilled the Divine promise then, teaching us that Redemption could come again.

For the individual who may be mired in the dregs of daily living, the promise is all the more important: God will redeem you, just as God delivered those in the past.

# Chapter Twenty-Three

## Shulḥan Orekh: Feeling Sustained

*Dinner is finally served, and we are grateful for the abundant harvest of which we can take part. There are multiple courses and generally much more food than we can eat. The meal is sumptuous, but we miss its point if we don't allow it to pale in comparison to the simple foods that we have eaten from the seder plate. We need food to sustain us, but without an ongoing relationship with God, we remain starved.*

### Preparation

This evening's meal is all about preparation, for it is not the kind of dinner that you throw together at the last minute. In the midst of preparing the transition to Pesaḥ for the entire household, we also have to plan an extensive dinner for an abundance of people. It's a tricky business, this preparing for weeks in advance a meal that is *pesaḥdik*, and at the same time cleaning up the *ḥametz* throughout the house. The task demands a lot of juggling—for everyday life continues at its hectic pace. Then comes the other big question: where to fit all of our guests?

Some people have different needs when they consider purchasing a new home. They investigate the schools, the proximity to synagogues, the convenience to shopping and perhaps public transportation. The list goes on, but if you are like most, you also want to consider the configuration of the dining room and adjacent areas. How many tables and chairs can you fit into an expanded dining area? Many of my friends leave an extra place or two around the table when planning: You never know who'll you'll meet in shul just before the holiday, even that day. We express our appreciation for what we have received by sharing our bounty with others because we understand that it is all ours only temporarily. Will there be room enough to share your bounty in this way? Will the kitchen accommodate all of your Passover needs? All this for an extended week once a year. But that's the power of this holiday. So we prepare for this meal even when Pesaḥ is months away. And that's what is significant about this holiday.

## Davar Aḥer

Once we finally get to the meal—even though it is late in the evening, the kids are cranky, and some of the relatives who are unfamiliar with the progress of the seder are antsy—we should be conscious of the nurturing sustenance of God. It is too easy to rush into the meal and just eat. So even now we begin slowly with an egg in salt water (symbolizing the spring festival that we anxiously sought to leave Egypt to celebrate, the circle of life, and the residual bitterness of slavery). Before we are ready to express our appreciation and our thanks, we have to take stock of our blessings and acknowledge them to ourselves. I like to go around the table and introduce everyone at this point in the seder. It drives some guests crazy because they have been following the pages in the haggadah, flipping ahead when they thought no one was looking, taking quick peeks at their watches. But this is not your typical introduction, for people have already said hello to one another before we even sat down. Instead, I introduce them by way of saying aloud what each person means to me, how I am thankful for the miracles that they have brought into my life: my wife, our children, our friends and neighbors, whomever we have invited to join us for the seder. And then I invite people to do the same. Sometimes it is an awkward few minutes or so, but eventually at least one brave soul enters the water—and then others more boldly follow.

The meal may get a little cold (or perhaps a little overcooked), although my family is used to the circuitous routes that I have a penchant for taking. I have always believed that time has no place in the midst of celebration. If we can attend meetings that go on and on in our pursuit of community, then we can certainly participate in one or two ritual meals that go on and on in pursuit of historical memory. Then we finally eat, and in doing so we come to realize that the food and the people who join us in eating it sustain us in ways that we never thought possible.

# Chapter Twenty-Four

## Tzafun: Finding the Hidden Self

*For many, searching for the afikoman is a childhood game, given over to the younger people who sit around the seder table. Though various communities differ as to the rules (and as to how the "found" afikoman is ransomed), some overlook the primary lesson. The afikoman reminds us that there is a hidden part of the self that yearns to be found and revealed. It may lie hidden beneath the experience of slavery, but now we should feel free to reveal it.*

### Preparation

The telling of the story of the Passover helps lead us toward a greater sense of wholeness. We have purged from our souls that which clutters our lives. What was broken has been made whole, even if just for the time being. We have filled our minds, our souls, and our stomachs. What was lost can now be found. Some would argue that this journey exists only in the religious imagination and not in reality. I would suggest that our religious imagination is our most important reality. Rabbi Ira Stone teaches that the place where God and human being meet is the imagination.[1] The imagination, which classic Jewish philosophy often denigrates, is raised to sacred proportions by Stone. But the Passover experience is not limited to even that sense of the imagination. It occurs in very concrete ways in the reality of our lives. While most people relegate spirituality to the intangible, preparing for Passover creates openings for real cleaning in which spiritual change and growth can take place.

Like the *afikoman* hidden at the beginning of the seder and recovered only after the retelling of the story so that our deliverance is complete, there are parts of ourselves that remain hidden and require time for searching out and recovery. Our secular culture promotes therapy, jogging, and travel as means to discover the inner self, to name just a few of the current trends. They may help and may even work unaided. However, oftentimes these activities need a spiritual lens to focus our heart and our soul. So I recommend journal writing, meditation, and prayer as accompanying activities. The preparation for Passover itself can also provide us with a window to peer into our souls. As Passover approaches, consider the parts of yourself that you would like more present in your daily life. Examine that hidden part of you longing to be artist or athlete, writer or cook, lover or parent, sibling or friend. Take the time before Passover to experiment with those parts of yourself. Now that we are free, each of us should engage in the activities that bring out our concealed parts. In this way, you will also find the *afikoman* and return it back to the table without even leaving your chair. When they thought they could not pass, God brought the Israelites through the Red Sea and when they thought they would die, God led them through the desert. These deeds God carried out so that they could be full and free human beings in the Land of Israel—so that *we* could taste freedom and fulfillment.

### Davar Aḥer

Sometimes the matzah breaks into more pieces than we anticipated. We try to divide it into pieces for our guests, but it seldom breaks the way we planned. We think that with machine-made, mass-produced matzah that is scored for breaking, we should be able to evenly distribute the matzah, but it is an impossible task. *Shemurah matzah* does not even try to pretend; because of the way it is made, its shape is uneven and inconsistent. There is no way you are going to break this matzah easily, so why bother? (It was not so easy to break up the cycle of slavery either.) While we would prefer a neat, compartmentalized world, matzah reminds us that the distinctions in our lives are not so clearly discernible. While we are all the same on one level, created in the image of the Divine, we also are all different. As the rabbis noted, when we make a mold for a coin, each one is cast the same. However, in the Divine cast of the human each one is essentially the same but existentially different.

When the *afikoman* is reunited with what remains of the piece of matzah, we have a sense that the missing piece of matzah serves to make us whole. As the missing piece of matzah is joined to its other half, make a mental list of those pieces that you are working to bring back together. Imagine the pieces of yourself being combined once again to form the self you once were and the self you are yet to be. Then take a bite of the *afikoman*. It will taste quite different.

# Chapter Twenty-Five

## *Barekh:* Giving Thanks for How Far We Have Come

> Regardless of the obstacles we have encountered, God
> helps us to overcome them, just as God did with our
> ancestors in ancient Egypt. So we are grateful. And
> we express our thanks by saying "God is good and
> God causes goodness in the world." We say these
> words aloud to make sure that we, ourselves, can hear
> the words.

### Preparation

During holidays (and on the Sabbath), we begin Grace after Meals (*Birkat ha-Mazon*), the prayer of thanksgiving, with a psalm (Ps. 126). As is the case with other psalms, one of our ancestors found a way to poetically say in words what we long to express, the yearning of our hearts. We are over-flowing with gratitude, although words cannot reflect the depth of our thanks. Our response, however inadequate, is an expression of profound appreciation to God for the overwhelming love that God has shared with us.

The psalm reminds us that our return to Zion feels like a dream. But the return to the Land of Israel is a fulfillment of our dream. It is a sentiment that courses through the blood of each individual Jew. Of course, we are thankful to God for our return to Zion, but dreams transcend even the sacredness of that land. They reflect what we can ultimately become and are part of the vision we set for ourselves. One teacher, Rabbi Samuel Kalman Mirsky, taught that if dreams are to be realized they must be what he calls "dreams of the dawn." These are dreams of Redemption. They are dreams of affirmation, dreams of inspiration and hope—for these are the dreams out of which Jewish destiny is made. These dreams have a practical dimension that humans can help make real. Such was the case with the building of the modern state of Israel, and such is the case with the ultimate Redemption of the Jewish people—which is the dream whose image is captured in the psalm. What do you dream for yourself for Pesah this year? I have one colleague who always wants to know of people he meets, "What are you dreaming about right now?"

### Davar Aḥer

Our thanks to God takes many forms in *Birkat ha-Mazon*. There are several components to this prayerful expression of gratitude. After the introductory psalm that is recited on special occasions like Pesah, we join together in an invitation to prayer. After all, someone has to remind those who are sitting around the table, talking and shmoozing, that it is time to focus their attention on expressing thanks to God—even though they just finished singing or reciting of a psalm. Such singing can be raucous and loud and even unfocused. Most of all, when such joy overflows the heart, as is the case with this psalm, the behaviors that follow may be unpredictable. We need to be called back to the task. For genuine prayer to take place, we need to focus our attention. This is what real *kavanah* is all about.

While *Birkat ha-Mazon* can be said by an individual who sits alone, there are certain requirements when saying it with a group. Since it is appropriate to say *Birkat ha-Mazon* from the place where you have eaten (or, as some say, so that you can see the place where you have eaten), if you have been making the rounds with your Passover guests, moved into another room in the house, or switched places with another, now is the time to hurry back—if you've not done so already. When three people are present, a liturgical invitation must be issued. And when ten people are present (sufficient for a prayer quorum, a minyan, depending on your custom), then God's name must be added.

There are four blessings, four expressions of our thanksgiving, that are articulated in the prayer. They represent for us different viewpoints for our thanks. The first three blessings emerge from the Bible. First, we acknowledge God as the Source of all that sustains us. Second, we thank God for the blessing of the land with an understanding that it is upon this land that we grow food for sustenance and nourishment. The third blessing is for the building of Jerusalem and its return to our hearts as the spiritual capital of the world. While it is true that one is obligated to orient oneself in prayer toward Jerusalem, the poet Yehudah ha-Levi once said that the obligation is to turn one's heart in prayer to Jerusalem.

The final blessing comes from the rabbis rather than the Bible. It is referred to as *Ha-tov ve-ha-mativ* (for the good and for the One [God] who causes goodness). This fourth blessing was introduced into the *Birkat ha-Mazon* prayer directly following the unsuccessful Bar Kokhba rebellion. Perhaps it was a way of reaffirming the future of the Jewish people when their hopes for Redemption (through Shimon bar Kokhba as their leader) were dashed. This final prayer reflects a very powerful sentiment that the Jewish people have struggled with in their relationship to God throughout its history. The tension in the relationship is apparent. We want to believe in the goodness of God and in the justice of God's actions in the world, but we see evidence that seems to contradict it. So we continue to look for goodness as a way of buoying our faith in God and our optimism for the world. This seder prayer encourages us to believe. And it supports our desire to develop a meaningful relationship with God.

How does one develop a relationship with a God who is fully unknowable? We try to understand who God is and what God wants of us. This endeavor is particularly important when Jewish blood is spent, though we say that when lives are lost, they are for *kiddush ha-Shem,* the sanctification of God's name (read: reputation). That is why the tradition *requires* us to say aloud—even in the face of tragedy—that God *is* good and *causes* good. Though we may have experienced many Egypts in our lives, we are taught to remember through the seder that God continues to deliver us from them. Although there are historians who maintained a pessimistic interpretation of Jewish history, this blessing helps us move beyond the tragic, taking us forward, on the way to messianic times.

# Chapter Twenty-Six

## Welcoming the Promise of Elijah

*The prophet Elijah is the personification of optimism, particularly because he is said to be the one who will herald the messianic era. As a result, he is an ever welcome guest in our midst, particularly on holidays when our moods are elevated and our homes are filled with joy. His presence is a symbol of God's promise to deliver us.*

### Preparation

The prophet Elijah is an old friend to Jewish memory, so much so that European Jewish folk legend is filled with miracle stories about him. In our memory, he has traveled with us as we have journeyed through history. He has been our hero, our protector, our confidante. We invite him into our homes on various specific occasions, as well. Every Saturday night, we make mention of Elijah during *Havdalah*. In that time of darkness, as the light of Shabbat slips behind the trees and we lose hold of it, Elijah reminds us of the ultimate light that will sweep away the darkness. He joins us at the *brit milah*, when our promise for the future—a newborn son—is linked with the destiny of the Jewish people and entered into a covenantal relationship with God. Likewise, we save a place for Elijah at the seder table. Elijah's presence is a sign of our optimism, for he alone will usher in *mashiaḥtzeit*, the time of the Messiah. This is particularly poignant in the passage following the final blessing of *Birkat ha-Mazon*, whose inclusion was provoked by the failure of the Bar Kokhba rebellion and the large number of Jews whose lives were lost during the revolt. Again we see in the ritual inclusion of Elijah the amazing resilience of the Jewish people, who in the midst of defeat and despair respond with a hope that knows no bounds. This hope spills over into our individual lives as well. Contained in the cup, therefore, is a prescription for personal happiness.

Sometimes, as we prepare for the seder, things emerge that previously remained under the surface of our relationships, particularly with family and friends. They remind us of past hurts and conflicts that have gone unresolved. Rather than waiting for them to color the seder experience, embrace them so that you can attend to them ahead of time. Pick up the telephone. Take a drive. Do what is necessary to confront the potential for conflict before it erupts. Then you can welcome Elijah to the table with open arms and a full heart.

### Davar Aḥer

There is some debate in the Talmud as to whether or not a fifth cup of wine should be consumed at the seder, given that the Torah contains this fifth promise of Redemption: "And I will bring you into the land" (Exod. 6:8). The sages deferred the decision pending the arrival of the prophet Elijah, who would pass the final decision on this ritual decision. Thus, the wine is poured (into what has been come to be called Elijah's Cup), but it is not consumed. This is more than ritual "compromise" among the rabbis. The presence of the cup of Elijah emphasizes the essential element of optimism that pervades the seder and provides the rhythmic foundation for the entire holiday calendar.

Some people play games with this cup of wine, drinking it quickly while children have left the table to open the door for Elijah. It is the custom in some families to fill the cup of Elijah with a bit of wine from each cup on the table, symbolically suggesting that we agree to have a role in ushering in the messianic era.

As the conversation evolves around the seder table, it naturally moves from the particular subjects described in the haggadah to the events in our community that resonate with the salient issues to which the rabbis direct our attention. It is easy to dismiss some of the global subjects as those that we cannot influence. However, the cup of Elijah teaches us that we can make a difference in everything—as long as we believe we can.

# Chapter Twenty-Seven

## *Hallel:* Singing Songs of Praise

*Sometimes simple words express all that there is to say: Thank you God. Thank you for all that You did for our ancestors and for all that You have done for me and for all that You are yet to do. With these words of thanks, we near the conclusion of the seder.*

### Preparation

Most children, when they are very young, like to sing. At an early age, we frequently tell them to be quiet, to sing softly, not to disturb other people. And if we don't, someone else is bound to do so at school or at play. Then we socialize children into thinking that some people have better voices than others, so many refrain from singing aloud. (Some continue to sing in the shower or bath, when they are alone.) And then they (we) become teenagers and everything is at risk—though some use music as a guide through the turbulent teenage years. After adolescence the lucky few are able to reclaim their early desires to sing. For others, the window was closed so tightly that it takes a great effort to reopen it. That is why the Hallel psalms are so important to spiritual growth. These words are carried heavenward on the wings of song—and they have the ability to carry us along with them.

I like to sing. While it bothers me that I do not have a particularly good voice, I have never let it get in my way—even when people have looked askance at my desire to sing. And I like to sing loudly. I always considered the ability (and desire) to sing as a gift from God, so I use it. When I sing, I am able to hear what my heart yearns to say. It reflects my profound beliefs, and so I want others to hear. Thus, when I have an opportunity to sing praises to God, I do so. Hallel provides us with an opportunity to sing out.

There are many ways to praise God and there are many ways to sing.

Cantor Benjie Ellen Schiller once asked me why I was not singing when she was leading us in community prayer. She knew such silence in the midst of song was an unusual posture for me. I assured her that I was singing—but silently. Not all songs burst forth across the lips. Sometimes the most moving Hallel songs are sung in silence.

### Davar Aḥer

In contexts other than the seder, Hallel is sung during the day. Like so much of the seder, our ritual behaviors challenge the norm. They set a new standard for routine. So it is not entirely surprising that during the seder we sing Hallel even though it is nighttime. The rabbis suggest that this exception is made because the deliverance of the Israelites took place at night. Some people have used this idea to lend further support to the notion that the Jewish people are a people of the moon, because we left Egypt (and other countries) in the darkness of the night, our way lit only by the moon and stars. Maybe the Hallel is permitted at night for the seder because the rabbis recognized that we are more afraid at night than during the day. Fear is a natural response to darkness. Children are often afraid to go to sleep at night, so we leave a little light on for them to see by. Perhaps we leave the bedroom door ajar. And when our children are very young, we may even leave an electronic monitor in the room to listen to them—and so they are reassured that we are looking after them even if we are not actually in the room with them. When we acknowledge God with Hallel, we also recognize that God's light provides a path for us in the darkness of the night—and of our lives.

The Hallel is divided somewhat in the seder. This too is unusual. Two of its paragraphs are recited before the meal. Most scholars explain this division as a way of relating the early sections of the Hallel psalms with the sections of the haggadah read before the meal, both of which focus on the Exodus. Like the latter sections of the haggadah that are read after the meal, the latter part of Hallel focuses on future Redemption. There is also a practical reason. Conscious of liturgical aesthetics, the rabbis placed each cup of wine into a textual context. Since the second cup of wine had no textual backdrop, the rabbis used the text of the early part of Hallel to give that cup the context it needed. Perhaps, however, the meal is a transition between the Exodus and our Redemption. When we were slaves, we were not fully sustained. But as part of our Redemption, we have come to recognize the extent to which God nourishes our body and our soul.

# Chapter Twenty-Eight

## Nishmat Kol Ḥai: Every Soul Can Be Renewed

*Praised. Extolled. Acclaimed. Hallowed. Glorified.*
*These words of praise do not even approximate what*
*we want to express about God, particularly once we*
*have experienced the Divine in our own midst. We*
*experience the Divine through each breath we take.*
*And with each breath, we offer thanks. Nishmat Kol*
*Ḥai is a prayer poem that also makes its way into the*
*prayer book on Shabbat and holidays.*

### Preparation

What does one do to ensure the renewal of the soul? Is it a matter of going
to sleep early at night, getting regular exercise, reading the right books, listening to the best music, praying regularly? What is it? First we have to recognize that each individual has a soul, and then we must be convinced that
the soul of the individual—darkened through years of slavery—can be
renewed. Next we have to begin the process of readying our soul for the
renewal that comes with the dawn of a new day—which is symbolized by
the move from slavery to freedom.

Just as we ready ourselves for a marathon, successively increasing our distance and our speed, we should do the same for the seder. The value of
endurance is particularly evident toward the end of the seder, just like the
real test of our stamina emerges toward the end of the race.

So I invite those of you who don't make prayer part of your daily routine
to begin praying regularly. Some may prefer to start with the traditional
rubrics of prayer. After weeks, months, and then years of daily prayer, we can
fully appreciate what is indeed a fixed spiritual practice. Others may start
more basically by simply isolating a few minutes each day (working up to

three times a day) to gather their thoughts and direct them toward something greater than themselves, which our tradition has named God. To build on this relationship, we employ rituals. These rituals help bridge the gap we may feel between ourselves and God or, perhaps, nurture the relationship that has already been started. Then, when we get to the seder, even if the rituals and prayers themselves are unfamiliar, the framework for doing them is not.

We use the very substance of our being—the soul—to relate to God, for it is in the soul that we can best understand how we are created in the image of God.

### Davar Aḥer

At the conclusion of this section introduced by *Nishmat Kol Ḥai*, the editors of the haggadah use fifteen different expressions to praise God. Fifteen represents many things, including the number of major sections of the seder until this point (from *Kaddesh* until *Nirtzah*). What are the fifteen ways that you are prepared to praise God in the midst of your family celebration of Pesaḥ during the seder? Think of the words and then what you might do to express them. Start with the words presented in the haggadah. It's obvious that the words themselves (whose nuanced meanings may make it hard to discern one from the next) are part of an ongoing list to get you started, to help provide you with a posture, so you can then continue on your own.

These words of Hallel praise are repeated in the synagogue throughout Passover, just as they are at the table these first nights—helping us to understand the relationship between both houses, both homes. When we run out of words, when there is nothing left to say, when nothing can convey what it is that we have to say to God, we simply breathe, deeply and resolutely. For in our breath is our commitment to life. In our breath is our optimism for the future. In our breath is praise for the God who first gave us breath and who will one day remove it from us, as well.

Some say this is all that was really heard at Sinai—the wind that rushes in the throat to create language, the wind that it takes to create the first word of the ten utterances (Ten Commandments): *Anokhi*, I. I alone am God who gives you breath. So breathe deeply and live. Breathe deeply and come closer to Me.

# Chapter Twenty-Nine

## Nirtzah: Acceptance

*Even before the seder, and now at its end, we pray that the words we have offered will be accepted by God. Moreover, we make a commitment that the prayers that have been said will be affirmed by the deeds we perform. The soulful acts that follow the seder will reflect the preparation we are making beforehand.*

### Preparation

We want our prayers to be accepted by God. That's why the seder combines joyful celebration with hard work. Important things do not come so easily. So after this rich experience, we pray that our words may be accepted, hoping that they have been carried heavenward on the wings of the seder rituals. In order to ensure that our prayers will indeed be heard by the Almighty—and it is a bit presumptuous to even consider that we have the power to force God's hand, so to speak—we acknowledge that we also have to work to transform our lives into lives of prayer. Words that are unaccompanied by deeds are hollow. If the days following the seder become much the same as the days that preceded it, then the rituals of the seder and all of the preparation for Pesah may have been for naught. Just as we want God to be accepting of us, *we* have to be accepting of ourselves as well. So in preparation for the seder, we strive to do the best we can, then reach deeper to do better without beating ourselves up in the process.

Holidays give us pause to consider many things in our lives because, for a short while, we take ourselves out of our regular routine. And given that Passover requires such extensive preparation, it takes us out of our regular routine for a period of time extending beyond the parameters of the days of the holiday itself. But the extra time is not limited to the days and weeks before the first seder. It must also include those moments after the last piece of matzah has been eaten—for at Passover's end, most people rush to find the first piece of *hametz* they can get their hands on. In traditional neighborhoods this is difficult because *hametz* can't even be baked until after the holiday has concluded. It is tradition's way of saying, "You spent so much time purging yourself of *hametz,* don't rush so quickly to accumulate it once again in your soul." Most people assume that this is about ritual law. Rather, such legal requirements were enacted out of a deep spiritual concern for the people.

So what will you do in preparation for the holiday to ensure that you are able to keep your soul free of *hametz* even after the last hours of Pesah have passed?

### Davar Aher

By this time, the food has helped to temper the effect of the first three glasses of wine. We now fill the glass to the top, allowing the wine (or grape juice) to overflow slightly (and stain the cloth beneath it—unless you remember to place a tray somewhere under the cup) in order to express our overflowing joy. But we are careful not to pour too much, for that would undermine our sense of humility and gratitude. Joy is precious, and we do not want to waste it frivolously. With our right hand, we raise the glass of wine heavenward once again. We extend the right arm, recognizing it is the arm of strength, imitating the arm of God that brought us out of Egypt, strong and outstretched. Just as we have held the previous three cups of wine, we hold this cup in the palm of our hand, so that it sits like a flower opening its blossom of beauty, reaching its head to the sun, striving to bring beauty to the world as it lifts itself toward its Source.

With the fourth cup of wine, we are able to finally understand the symbolism that the wine has carried throughout the seder, equal in importance to matzah. The Psalmist expresses it for us: "You plucked a vine out of Egypt…and You planted it. You cleared a place for it so that it took root and filled the land" (Ps. 80:9–10). The seder wine begins as grapes on the vine. And through crushing and careful processing, and by undergoing remarkable change, the wine is able to bring joy to the heart (although we must always be sensitive to those for whom wine brings pain, not joy). Wine can soothe and soften. And here it is raised to the level of sacred. We experienced this same process along with our people as slaves in Egypt—just as we now bless the wine, God blessed our people, lifting us toward our Source and to freedom.

Prayer is a challenging experience. It takes discipline and depth. We call this mix *keva* and *kavanah*. Whether we are speaking about the regular discipline of daily prayer or the spontaneous outpouring of the heart, we don't know whether our prayers will be accepted. But we pray nevertheless and hope that we are heard.

# Chapter Thirty

## Le-Shanah ha-Ba'ah be-Yerushalayim:
## Visions of Jerusalem

*No matter how far away the Jewish people have trav-
eled or for how long, and now even as we live in the
Land, Jerusalem remains the dream of the Jewish
people. Jerusalem is the prism through which we see
the entire world. It is the center of all that we do and
all that we think. And if we close our eyes and breathe
deeply, we can easily be transported there.*

### Preparation

Only after we have acknowledged the offerings of our own souls can we
move to the next level of pre-Pesaḥ spirituality: imagining the most perfect
future. Ever since the time of Abraham and Sarah, and later after the return
to Zion following Egyptian slavery, the Jewish people have imagined living
in Jerusalem. Jerusalem represents a closeness to God in space and the possibility of living in a state of pure holiness. Jerusalem is more than a special
place; it is holy space. This return to Jerusalem is often understood as the
messianic era, a time of ultimate Redemption for the entire world. Rabbi
Abraham Kook saw it this way: "Would that all of our children standing now
on the threshold of the upcoming Redemption listen and recognize its noble
objective and know that our current efforts and yearnings are necessary to
enable us to bind the distant, bygone Redemption with Redemption of the
future....We are summoned to stand before the entire world with a pure,
refined soul which appears in its full glory on the stage of the world, to shine
as an everlasting beacon for all the nations under the heavens....This is the
attribute that binds the Pesaḥ of Egypt with the Pesaḥ of the future."[1]

Jerusalem is ever present in the life of the spirit. Like the smashing of a
glass at the conclusion of a Jewish wedding ceremony, which reminds us of

the endless hope for Redemption, we again transport ourselves to Jerusalem at the end of the seder. Both the wedding and the seder are experiences in which we can act on our intense faith in the future.

In moving toward the end of Passover, the possibility of a climax of joy awaits us. Rabbi Ira Stone says it this way: "Joy is the experience of well-being that comes with love that is properly received." If we properly receive the experience of love through the possibility of wholeness and Redemption during Passover, then we can feel intense joy. "The goal of religious life," adds Rabbi Stone, "is to enable us, in this world, to taste the joy of the world-to-come as fully as possible."[2] Allowing ourselves temporarily to experience what awaits us in our final return to Jerusalem, when we will be made whole once again—even for those who travel to physical Jerusalem rather frequently or even live there—helps us to experience the joy of being whole in this life. Of Jerusalem we have dreamed. For Jerusalem we will wait.

### Davar Aḥer

The climax of the seder experience can be expressed in four simple words: "Next year in Jerusalem." After the experience of the seder, we are able to imagine ourselves in Jerusalem next year participating in our final Redemption. The abstract "tomorrow" is made into the concrete of "next year." This idea transforms the seder from a "this world" experience to a "next world" journey. Jerusalem is more than just a definition of boundaries (albeit under constant dispute) on a plot of land; it is a state of mind that transcends the limits of time and geography. At the same time, we recognize that the values that have marked and maintained our people must begin in Jerusalem. "From Zion will (indeed) Torah go forth, and God's word from Jerusalem" (Isa. 2:3). So Jerusalem—beginning with our seder table—becomes a laboratory for the institution of these values. Jerusalem is the center of our spiritual world.

Some people choose to sing "Hatikvah" at this point in the seder as a reminder that Israel offers us the possibility of bringing the messianic era forward, rooted in the journey of our people. As we insisted on our freedom from Egypt, we modern Jews insist on our freedom today and on the right to an independent homeland that is flush with Jewish values. Only when we see ourselves as personally and collectively responsible for our fate there can we be truly free.

Such freedom depends first on a vision of what might be. It also is determined by the strength of one's will to implement the vision. Theodor Herzl said, "If you will it, it is not a dream!" If we work toward it, we can make the ideal real. Justice Louis Brandeis took Herzl's notion a little further. He suggested that many peoples dream, but what is unique about the Jewish people is its uncanny ability to realize its dreams. If your will is strong, if your hope is deep, if you are committed to the continuous process of perfecting yourself (by becoming fully human) and making your life whole, then you can transform any dream you have for yourself into reality.

# Chapter Thirty-One

## Anticipating Revelation:
## Moving from Passover to Shavuot

*The Jewish year begins before Pesaḥ and continues
after it. Our challenge is to synchronize the personal
journey of discovery with the year's rhythm. While
there are a variety of points along the way that make
entry a little easier, the time period that we mark from
Pesaḥ to Shavuot helps move us along from liberation
to Revelation and on our way to Redemption.*

While the experience of Passover is never really complete, at its conclusion each year we come closer to the final Redemption that it directs us toward. As Rabbi Melvin Glazer often reminds me on Shabbat, particularly at the end of a rough week for both of us: we are one day closer to the messianic era. It is one of the reasons why Passover has been the foundational event for the Jewish people throughout our history. It helps us to understand each year in a more profound way that the real purpose of Jewish history is more than just the recording of events over time. According to Rabbi Abraham Isaac Kook, "The Redemption continues. The Redemption from Egypt and the complete Redemption in the future are one continuous act of God's strong hand and outstretched arm. They began to operate in Egypt and continue to act in all subsequent events."[1] So we continue the journey toward personal and world Redemption, fully knowing that there will be stops along the way.

Each year, as we bring to a close our personal observance of the Passover holiday, we work to fully integrate the experience of the Exodus into the multidimensional, multilayered experiences of our lives. Every Passover, each personal Exodus, contributes to who we are and what we have—and will—become. Through this annual process of going forth from slavery

89

toward freedom, new opportunities to lift our souls closer to Heaven present themselves before us. It's part of the process of spiritual logic. The very ingredient that is designed to cause bread to rise actually weighs us down. *Ḥametz* in the soul creates an illusion for us. It may cause dough to rise, but there is no real substance to it.

Now that we have worked to rid ourselves of the *ḥametz* that puffed up our souls and, as a result, have attempted to make peace with the enslavements of the past, we are prepared to hold the image of a perfected world in our minds and work toward it. Breathing a sigh of relief, it seems impossible to return to the narrow places of Egypt now that we have tasted the unparalleled joys of newfound freedom. But we must be ever vigilant. Potential enslavements constantly threaten us. Not recognizing this reality is perhaps the greatest danger we face as we make our way through the desert of our lives on our way to the Promised Land.

Whatever we experience, whatever encounter we have had, whatever relationship we have known can never be fully forgotten. It makes its mark on our souls. As with Egypt, we can never fully leave any experience behind us. And we pass it on to our children as if they too had lived through it. Each experience becomes part of our personal story, as it does our collective story as a people. These experiences help shape who we have become. Thus, like the Israelites who carried with them the broken shards of the first tablets that Moses shattered, along with the whole ones in the Ark of the Covenant, we must carry the burdens of our past into the future.

There are three primary prisms through which we can review our journey and gain perspective on it. These three prisms are refracted throughout the historical experience of the Jewish people. They mark each stage in our history, no matter where we have lived, no matter what we have done. Each idea—Creation, Revelation, and Redemption—supports a central way of viewing the world and our purpose in life. Without any one of them, the possibility of seeing ourselves as participants in the ongoing evolution of humanity—as God's covenantal partners—is impossible.

Creation provides us with the fundamental sense of what it means to be a human being, created in God's image, within the context of the Creation of the earth and every living thing. We could not exist without the idea of Creation. We relive this notion of Creation both as we awaken each day and once weekly during Shabbat, when we see the world re-created, as we are, anew. Revelation provides us with a roadmap for our journey to Redemption and the tools we need to bring it into reality. That is why it must be experienced on the concrete dimension of the Land. Revelation is the climax of the Israelites' journey to the Land of Israel and serves as the bridge between Creation and Redemption. However, we cannot be fully human without the notion of Redemption, which is as much an essential ingredient as birth itself.

## Counting of the Omer

We have a tendency to count down those things we anticipate. Some people have a calendar and mark each day with an X as they move closer toward their goal. For some, that goal is the completion of an educational program; for others, it is simply a vacation. For still others, it is the day on which they will be reunited with their loved ones after a period of separation. Addicts in recovery mark off the minutes, hours, and days of their sobriety and rightfully celebrate each one as moments of rebirth and renewal. In our family, we mark off the days since Sheryl's last cancer surgery. Each day is a blessing for which we are grateful.

For the Jewish people, the period between Passover and Shavuot represents such a period of time. While it is true that our people encountered God throughout their journey in the desert, after they experienced Revelation at Sinai they longed for it again. And so, each year, we count down the time from the Exodus at Passover (starting with the second night) until the night before Shavuot, when God revealed the Torah to the Jewish people. This period of forty-nine days represents the time from the cutting of the first barley sheaves through the end of the grain-harvesting season. Flour from those first sheaves was brought to the Temple and presented as a grain offering, an Omer. During the time when the First (and later the Second) Temple stood, this provided us with a special opportunity to express our gratitude to God for a bountiful harvest—and all that it implies.

In ancient days, this period of time appeared to be filled with joy. As our people moved through history and encountered forms of slavery once again, the counting of the Omer assumed a more somber tone, as its timbre was shaped by the rabbis. Slowly, people added on layers of observance that deepened its seriousness. Rituals of mourning characterized this period as weddings and haircuts were prohibited, except on the thirty-third day (Lag ba-Omer), when, according to tradition, the plague that threatened the lives of Rabbi Akiva's students stopped. It is entirely possible that this "plague" really referred to the decimation of Akiva's students by the Romans following Bar Kokhba's failed rebellion.

Many of us count down the days or even hours in anticipation of the arrival of a close friend. Moses Maimonides likens this to the counting of the forty-nine days from the anniversary of our departure from Egypt, to the anniversary of the Giving of the Torah. He contends that sole purpose for the deliverance of the Israelites from Egypt was the Revelation of the Torah. The mystics suggest that these forty-nine days are counted in order to mark the period of waiting between the deliverance of the Israelites from Egypt and their betrothal to the Torah at Sinai. So the counting is a kind of preparation for a deepening relationship between the Israelites and God. Such a relationship was only possible after we were delivered from Egypt.

During this period of time, we are able to reawaken and reclaim our primordial Jewish memory, as we shake off the remains of slavery that still cling to us after all these years. The Omer is a call to memory. Some mystics hold that there were forty-nine gates of purity that we passed through during our journey from Egypt to the Promised Land. And with each step forward, with each entry through a new gate, we were able to leave a little bit of slavery behind us. After being in Egypt for so long, it took a long time and a lot of work to shake off the experience of slavery, even for those in the new generation who heard only stories of Egypt and did not experience it firsthand. In our own lives, we each experience our personal slavery and personal liberation. Through each gate, we get closer to Sinai and closer to God.

### Shavuot

Those who thought Pesaḥ was a peak experience soon learn that during Shavuot the experience is even greater. Winter turns into spring. An edge is taken off the cold, but the summer sun is still a bit distant. The new identity that was forged at Pesaḥ is now more mature and ready for the ultimate encounter at Sinai. Like the weddings that have been delayed, resulting in weeks of tension and anxious anticipation, we await the great meeting (marriage) between God and Israel. The three primary festivals of the Jewish calendar—Sukkot, Passover, and Shavuot—lead us to a deep appreciation of a meaningful and secure existence in the world. During Sukkot, we huddle together in temporary dwellings. At Passover, we retrace our journey from slavery to freedom. And during Shavuot, we stay up all night studying the texts that have evolved from the one sacred text we are about to receive. We call this marathon *tikkun leil Shavuot*. This immersion in sacred literature helps to open us up to falling in love with the Jewish people and with God once again.

Many Sephardic congregations read aloud a poetic *ketubbah*, a marriage contract between God and the people of Israel. This document chronicles the passionate relationship that evolved between God and Israel, consummated in marriage as the experience at Sinai. In a rather interesting spin on the typically male-driven approach to Jewish tradition, collective Israel—and we as individuals—are personified as God's bride. While we may be critical of our ancestors for their frequent personification of God as male, it took a great deal of religious strength to see themselves collectively embodied as God's bride. And once we are wed to God, our relationship is indissoluble. So in the moments of Sinai, we bask in God's love. Quoting Rabbi Joseph D. Soloveitchik, who said that the Torah is a covenant of being, not of doing, Rabbi Yitz Greenberg explains: "The goal [of the Sinai experience on Shavuot] is the completion of being, the full realization of [our] humanness."[2] This is only possible in the context of the Covenant, an unparalleled expression of Divine love.

Thus, the ultimate preparation for Passover is that it is a primary step toward the Revelation of Sinai that is marked at Shavuot and replayed each time we read Torah aloud in community, each time we study the sacred text and enter into a dialogue with it. To prepare for Passover might take weeks, and its celebration might be over in a little more than a week. But its influence is felt throughout the entire year.

# Epilogue

## How Does the Journey to Freedom Continue?

How does the journey to freedom continue?
Following fire and cloud, we stumble,
shivering with cold and fear.
Some will always cry out to Egypt,
longing to return to the known.

How does the journey to freedom continue?
Risking together what we never imagined possible
on our own, we keep walking.
The sea rises to our nostrils.
Then, with a breath, the waters part.

How does the journey to freedom continue?
We build fragile shelters and watch as they sway in the wind.
Aching for song, our throats are parched.
The water is too bitter to drink.
Even manna sometimes tastes like sand.

But ours is a holy journey. We falter but will not turn back.
Embracing the challenge of tradition,
we clear new paths to the future.
Ours is a holy journey, a journey towards a new song.

TAMARA RUTH COHEN

# Glossary

*Ashkenazic:* Referring to those Jews descended from Germanic lands.

*Avodat Yisrael:* German prayer book edited by Seligman Isaac Baer in 1868; it included a scholarly commentary titled *Yakhin Lashon*. This edition became the standard for most subsequent prayer books.

*Bar Kokhba rebellion:* Led by Shimon bar Kokhba and supported by Rabbi Akiva. This unsuccessful rebellion against Rome took place in the years 132–135 C.E. Some people believed that this was the beginning of the messianic Redemption, with Bar Kokhba as the Messiah.

*bi'ur ḥametz:* The ritual of burning ḥametz.

*brit milah:* Ritual of circumcision.

*bubbe:* Yiddish for "grandmother."

*Elijah's Cup:* Ritual object placed on the seder table and filled with wine, as a sign of Redemption and the anticipation of the messianic era.

*golden mean:* A term used by philosophers to refer to the midpoint of balance between two polar extremes.

*goldene medina:* "Golden country"; how immigrants from Europe in the early part of the twentieth century referred to America.

*haggadah:* Literally, "the telling" of the story of the Passover; the book used to tell the story of the Exodus during the seder.

*halakhic:* Legal; from the word for Jewish law, *halakhah*.

*ḥametz:* Foods made with leaven, or yeast; also refers to the "puffiness" of our souls.

*ḥametzdik:* Ḥametz-like; from the Yiddish way of adding the suffix "-dik" (meaning "-like").

*hashkamah minyan:* Very early morning prayer service; "sunrise service."

**"Hatikvah":** Israel's national anthem; literally, "the hope."

*Havdalah:* The ritual that marks the separation between the holy and sacred nature of holiday time and the secular nature of daily life. At the end of the Sabbath, it is the ritual that includes a special candle, wine, and spice. During some other holidays, it is minimally marked simply by inserting a prayer into the *Amidah*, the core prayer, during the evening service.

**Holy One of Blessing:** Rabbinic euphemism for the name of God, also called the Holy Blessed One, or in gender specific-contexts (which I avoid throughout this book and in general), the Holy One, Blessed be He (*ha-Kadosh Barukh Hu*).

*Kaddish:* Prayer of affirmation that either separates parts of the service or is said exclusively by mourners. While each version is essentially the same, it can take one of a variety of forms depending on its use.

**kasher:** To make kosher or fit.

*kavanah:* A mantra of several words or a verse of sacred text used for meditative purposes; can also refer to the sacred intention with which you do something; it can also refer to spontaneous prayer, the polar opposite of *keva*, fixed prayer.

*Kedushah:* Prayer that is included only in the reader's repetition of the *Amidah* (see *Havdalah*, above), which requires a minyan, or a prayer quorum. The Reform movement has included it as part of the regular recitation of the *Amidah* and generally requires neither a reader's repetition nor a minyan.

*ketubbah:* Written marriage contract, often used as a metaphor for the Torah as the document that binds God to the Jewish people.

*keva:* Fixed or routine prayer, the polar opposite of *kavanah*, spontaneous prayer.

*Kiddush:* Prayer of sanctification usually said over wine (or grape juice).

*Kiddush Cup:* Ritual object used specifically for the reciting of *Kiddush.*

**Lag ba-Omer:** The thirty-third day of the Omer, a festival day of sorts, where the laws of the Omer are relaxed.

*Le-shanah ha-ba'ah be-Yerushalayim:* A toast of sorts, and an expression of messianic optimism, that concludes the seder (before the singing begins in earnest); literally, "To next year in Jerusalem." May we celebrate together there.

**Levites:** Descendents of Levi, the third son on Jacob. They were primarily the ones who assisted the priests in the ancient Temple in Jerusalem, although they were also gatekeepers, judges, teachers of the Law, and temple musicians.

*Likutei Moharan:* The collected teachings of Rabbi Naḥman of Bratzlav.

*mashiaḥtzeit:* From the Yiddish, "the time of the Messiah."

*me-avdut le-ḥerut:* "From slavery to freedom," a theme of Passover.

**mezuzah:** Literally, "doorpost"; refers to parchment that contains biblical verses that is affixed to the doorpost, marking the home as Jewish, related to the lamb's blood placed on the doorpost of Jewish homes to mark them so that the angel of death might pass over during the final plague.

**midrash:** Rabbinic interpretation, often made up of parables of primarily biblical material.

*mikveh:* Ritual bath used for immersion, particularly following menstruation and for conversion of men and women. Men often use the *mikveh* as a way of preparing for Shabbat and holidays.

**minyan:** Prayer quorum of ten. (According to traditional Judaism, this must be ten men. Reform, Reconstructionist, and many Conservative synagogues, however, count women among its number, as well.)

**Miriam's Cup:** Contemporary ritual object filled with water and placed on the seder table to remind us of the role of women in the Exodus from Egypt.

*Mitzrayim:* Egypt; literally "the narrow places."

**mitzvot:** Sacred obligations, commandments, Divine instructions.

*Modeh Ani:* Prayer of thanksgiving and acknowledgment said upon awakening in the morning.

**Nisan:** Hebrew month during which Pesaḥ occurs.

**Omer:** Period of time counted from the second evening of Passover until Shavuot, which was originally an agricultural marking period that has taken on nuances of mourning throughout Jewish history.

**Sabbath bride:** Personification of Shabbat by medieval mystics, who created liturgy and rituals to reflect this notion.

**seder:** Ritual evening meal for Passover, held on the first two nights in the traditional community and only on the first night in the liberal community, although a growing number of liberal Jews are now celebrating *sedarim* (plural of *seder*) on both nights. As is the case with all holidays except for Rosh Hashanah, only one night (and one seder) is observed in Israel.

**Sephardic:** Pertaining to those Jews who settled in Spain and whose descendants later scattered throughout Europe and the New World.

**Shavuot:** Spring harvest festival that celebrates the first fruits as well as the giving of the Torah on Mt. Sinai.

*shemurah matzah:* Matzah that has been carefully prepared from flour that was watched over from the time of the grain harvest (to prevent any measure of fermentation) and baked by hand.

**shmoozing:** Derived from the Yiddish word for socializing and conversation.

**shtetl:** Yiddish for a small village in Europe.

**Shulḥan Arukh:** The primary code of Jewish law. Also used here for its literal translation—a (properly) set table.

*simḥah:* A Hebrew term used to describe a happy family event such as a Bar or Bat Mitzvah or wedding.

**Sukkot:** Fall harvest festival that is celebrated by the building of (and temporarily living in) small booths or huts called *sukkot.*

**Talmud:** Oral law, eventually written down and compiled in 500 C.E. and made up of two sections: the Mishnah and Gemara. There are two Talmuds. One emerged in Babylonia and the other in the Land of Israel. They are referred to respectively as the Babylonian Talmud (BT), or Bavli, and the Jerusalem Talmud, or Yerushalmi.

*tikkun leil Shavuot:* Entire night of study on the eve of Shavuot.

**Tishrei:** Hebrew month during which Rosh Hashanah, Yom Kippur, and Sukkot take place.

*yetzer ha-ra:* The inclination to do evil; includes the various libidinal drives.

*yetzer ha-tov:* The inclination to do good.

*zeyde:* Yiddish for "grandfather."

**Zohar:** Core mystical text—a commentary on the Torah—in Judaism, from the Middle Ages, first published in 1295 in Guadalajara, Spain by Moses de Leon. De Leon ascribed its authorship to Rabbi Shimon bar Yochai, who lived during Hadrianic persecutions in the second century.

# *Personalities*

Rabbi Akiva (c. 50–135)—Famous sage of the Mishnah, known for his influence on the development of Jewish law. He became a scholar late in his life and had many students. Akiva was leader of a rabbinic academy and politically active in support of the Bar Kokhba revolt.

Shimon bar Kokhba (d. 135 C.E.)—Leader of the revolt against Rome (132–135 C.E.).

Naftali Zvi Yehuda Berlin (1817–1893)—Known by the initials of his name as ha-Netziv, one of the leading rabbis of his generation and head of the Volozhin Yeshivah in Lithuania for forty years.

Louis Brandeis (1856–1941)—The first Jew to be appointed as justice of the Supreme Court of the United States; active Zionist and Jewish communal leader.

Bratzlaver—A common diminutive form of the name Rabbi Naḥman of Bratzlav, taken from the city in which he lived.

Reuven P. Bulka (b. 1944)—Orthodox rabbi and founding editor of the *Journal of Psychology and Judaism*.

Tamara Ruth Cohen (b. 1971)—Composer. Consultant and former Program Director at Ma'ayan, the Jewish Women's Project affiliated with the JCC of the Upper West Side in New York.

Debbie Friedman (b. 1951)—Contemporary folk singer.

Neil Gillman (b. 1933)—Contemporary Conservative theologian and rabbi who is a professor of philosophy at the Jewish Theological Seminary of America.

Arthur Green (b. 1941)—Contemporary rabbi and scholar whose work focuses on Jewish mysticism; on the faculty of Brandeis University.

Tamara Green (b. 1944)—Chair of the Classics Department at Hunter College; serves on the board of the National Jewish Center for Healing.

Irving (Yitz) Greenberg (b. 1933) Contemporary Orthodox rabbi known for his vision and leadership, particularly in the founding of CLAL: The National Jewish Center for Learning and Leadership and the Jewish Life Network. He is also chair of the U.S. Holocaust Memorial Commission.

Yehudah Ha-Levi (1085–1141)—Medieval Spanish philosopher and poet; well-known author of *The Kuzari*.

Theodor Herzl (1860–1904)—Founder of modern political Zionism. His solution to anti-Semitism was the creation of a Jewish state which he described in the pamphlet *Der Judenstaat* ("The Jewish State").

Hillel (first century B.C.E.)—Talmudic sage born in Babylonia. He settled in the Land of Israel, where he was appointed president of the Sanhedrin. According to Hillel, the essence of Torah is contained in the following lesson: "Do not do unto others what is hateful to you. The rest is commentary. Go and learn it." Such was his directive to a potential convert who was challenged to learn Torah while standing on one leg.

Lawrence A. Hoffman (b. 1942)—Contemporary rabbi and liturgist, professor of liturgy at Hebrew Union College–Jewish Institute of Religion, and co–principal investigator for Synagogue 2000.

Abraham ibn Ezra (1097–1167)—Famous Spanish Jewish grammarian and Bible exegete. His commentaries were based on linguistic and factual examinations of the text and even included hints at foreshadowing.

Joshua of Kutno—Nineteenth-century east European rabbi who was known as an authority on *hametz*.

Ben Kamin (b. 1953)—Contemporary rabbi and author, formerly the spiritual leader of The Temple–Tifereth Israel in Cleveland, Ohio.

Abraham Isaac Kook (1865–1935)—Rabbi of Hasidic descent; educated at the Volozhin Yeshivah in Lithuania. He immigrated to the Land of Israel at the turn of the century. Rabbi Kook became chief rabbi of Jaffa and later first chief rabbi of what was then known as Palestine. His writings, infused with mystical teachings, stressed the centrality of Jewish nationalism and the Land of Israel.

Yerucham Leibovitz of Mir (d. 1936)—Rabbi and spiritual advisor (*mashgiah ruhani*) at the Mir Yeshivah.

Richard Levy (b. 1937)—Contemporary Reform rabbi who made his mark by championing the Pittsburgh Principles of 1999, which envisioned a warm approach to Jewish ritual, tradition, and observance.

Moses Chaim Luzzato (1707–1747)—Kabbalist and poet also known as Ramchal; head of center of Jewish learning in Padua, Italy. Luzzato had strong messianic aspirations and was exiled by the community's leadership to Amsterdam.

Moses Maimonides (1135–1204)—Also known as Moses ben Maimon and by the acronym Rambam. Maimonides is considered one of the greatest thinkers in all of Jewish history. Trained as a physician, he was also a commentator and philosopher. Under the influence of Aristotlean thought as articulated by the Arabic philosophers of the Middle Ages, he was best known for his *Guide for the Perplexed*, which caused a great deal of controversy, and his *Mishneh Torah*, an accessible compilation of Jewish law.

Malbim (1809–1879)—Initials for Meir Loeb Ben Yeḥiel Michael; rabbi, preacher, and biblical interpreter who eventually became chief rabbi of Romania.

Samuel Kalman Mirsky (1899–1967)—Scholar, religious Zionist, and Hebraist who taught at Yeshiva University and took an active role in the work of Mizrachi and Histadrut Ivrit of America.

Naḥman of Bratzlav (1772–1810)—Great-grandson of the Baal Shem Tov. One of the most influential Hasidic master teachers of the eighteenth century, he taught simple faith while emphasizing the importance of prayer and music.

Rav (third century c.e.)—Leading Babylonian teacher and founder of the academy at Sura.

Rachel Sabath (b. 1968)—Contemporary Reform rabbi, former faculty member at CLAL: The National Jewish Center of Learning and Leadership, and doctoral student at the Jewish Theological Seminary of America.

Samuel (end of second century to mid-third century)—Babylonian teacher. He was head of an important school and court at Nehardea.

Zalman Schacter-Shalomi (b. 1924)—Contemporary rabbi originally trained in the Lubavitch community; often credited as the driving force behind the movement for Jewish renewal.

Benjie Ellen Schiller (b. 1958)—Contemporary cantor and member of the faculty of the School of Sacred Music at Hebrew Union College–Jewish Institute of Religion in New York. She is also a member of the singing group Beged Kefet.

Sefat Emet—The pen name attributed to Yehudah Aryeh Leib Alter of Ger for the five volumes of his collected writings. He was the leader of the Ger Hasidim, one of the most celebrated sects of Hasidism and the largest in the modern state of Israel.

Joseph D. Soloveitchik (1903–1993)—Modern Orthodox rabbi, known as The Rav, who influenced generations of rabbis while on the faculty of the rabbinical school of Yeshiva University; well known for his seminal essay, "The Lonely Man of Faith."

Ira Stone (b. 1949)—Contemporary Conservative rabbi and author; spiritual leader of Temple Beth Zion–Beth Israel in Philadelphia.

Arthur Waskow (b. 1933)—Contemporary rabbi and author, leader in the Jewish renewal movement, and editor of the *New Menorah Journal*.

# Preparing the Seder

The Hebrew word *seder* means "order," and it is therefore the term that has come to be used to refer to the (home-based) festive meal, held on the first two nights of Passover, that follows a specific *order*. The paradigm for the seder emerges from an interpretation of Exodus 12:3–11 (which describes the last meal the Israelites prepared before leaving Egypt) and from the prescription repeated four times that urges parents to tell the story of the Exodus to their children (Ex. 12:26–27, 13:8, 13:14; and Deut. 6:20–21). The seder is divided into sections whose names identify the primary element ritualized in each section. (These classic divisions are marked in bold script in the table of contents in this book.) By the unusual disclosure of the rabbis, the seder follows the format of a Greek symposium and grants the participants the opportunity to become part of the elite of the nobility, if only for a short period of time. The seder uses real food to concretize all of the ideas that are implicit in the celebration and observance of Passover.

Participants take part in the seder while in a comfortable (leaning, reclining, slouching) position, particularly when drinking the required four cups of wine (or grape juice). Imitating royalty rather than reliving the experience of slaves, many people lean on a pillow during the seder. Generally, one leans to the left, which also keeps the esophagus open and permits the individual to drink with the right hand. In some medieval Sephardic communities, people enhanced the re-enactment of the seder by dressing for the journey. In order to add excitement to the contemporary seder, some families choose to do similar things today, often adding readings of current relevance. As a result, the haggadah (a book of narrative that takes participants through the story of the Exodus during the seder), even in the most traditional communities, is quite flexible and responsive.

While the seder begins after sunset, authorities grant some leeway to start the seder earlier should it be necessary to do so to accommodate young children. The table is set and the seder plate with its requisite symbolic elements is prepared. A shank bone (or a boiled beet if participants are vegetarian) is featured as the *zeroa* (literally, arm outstretched to sow seed), which represents the sacrificial lamb of the original Pesaḥ sacrifice. Alongside is a roasted egg (symbolic of a primitive springtime festival), which represents the *ḥagigah* (or festival) that the Israelites wanted the freedom (to leave Egypt) to celebrate. Other elements on the seder plate are the *maror* (bitter herb, usually horseradish), the *ḥaroset* (combination of chopped nuts, sweet wine, and fruit representing the mortar used by the ancient Israelites), and *karpas* (mildly bitter greens used to foreshadow the bitter herb and to encourage questions because of the odd nature of the ritual of dipping the vegetable in salt water before eating it). The green of the vegetable may also represent the spring and the promise of Redemption and the salt (water) may represent the sea as the mother of all life. The salt water is usually in a bowl since there's no special spot on the seder plate for it.

The seder follows a particular order. This order is usually sung aloud at the beginning of the seder or at various times during the seder as a mnemonic device and to help people follow along during the seder.

**Kaddesh:** This word comes from the Hebrew root that means "to make holy or separate" and refers to the *Kiddush* which is said over the first of four cups of wine (or grape juice). According to custom, one is supposed to drink at least half the cup, which should be filled to overflowing. In some homes only the leader chants the *Kiddush*. In many communities it is customary to stand while "making *Kiddush*," as it is called, and then sit while drinking.

**Ureḥatz:** This word is from the root meaning "to wash." The seder continues with the washing of hands in a prescribed ritual manner, but it is done without saying the blessing that usually accompanies this ritual act because no bread is to be eaten at this time. Washing is done by pouring water over each hand, alternating two or three times. While there are a variety of explanations for washing, it was an ancient custom to wash prior to dipping food in liquid.

**Karpas:** Next, greens (*karpas*) symbolic of spring are dipped in salt water and then eaten. Some rabbis suggest that the dipping is done to encourage the curiosity of the children. This allows for the explanation that the salt water is symbolic of the slaves' tears of bitterness. Others say to eat an amount equal to as much as half a potato, explaining this as a means either of counteracting the effect of drinking wine on an empty stomach or of temporarily satisfying one's hunger before the holiday meal is later served.

*Yaḥatz:* From the root meaning "to break or divide." We are breaking or dividing in half the middle of the three matzot that have been cere-monially placed on the table. One half is left for the *afikoman* (an obscure Greek loan word that refers to the piece of matzah to be found and eaten as "dessert" that might imply "take out the sweets" or "remove the dishes" so we can continue to celebrate or go elsewhere to cele-brate). This is covered and (in most families) hidden until later in the seder. In some communities, instead of sending off the children to find the *afikoman* later in the evening, they look for the opportunity to "steal" it and then offer it for "ransom" so that it can be shared as dessert. This was probably introduced to maintain the attention of the children throughout the seder. Yemenite Jews prohibit the "stealing" of the *afikoman*, because they consider it improper to even imitate the act of stealing.

*Maggid:* May be translated as "telling" or "narrating." Here we retell the bib-lical story of the Passover as it has been embellished by rabbinic com-mentary. The seder plate with its symbolic foods is lifted and the ceremonial matzot are briefly uncovered. This signifies the actual begin-ning of the haggadah, literally, the telling of the story. This makes up the long, middle section of the haggadah. The *Maggid* section contains many well-known elements such as the Four Questions, the Four Children (traditionally characterized as four *sons*), and the Ten Plagues. The sec-tion concludes with the drinking of the second cup of wine.

*Raḥtzah:* This word comes from the same root as *ureḥatz* and similarly means "washing." However, because this time the ritual will be followed by the eating of bread (or in this case, matzah), a blessing is said.

*Motzi, Matzah:* This combination of terms identifies God as the One "*who brings forth* bread from the earth" (*Motzi*). On Passover, it is the matzah that is brought forth. A double blessing of sorts, one for each element, is said over the matzah just prior to beginning the meal. Participants in the seder eat the matzah (but only the top and middle pieces of the three pieces of ceremonial matzot).

*Maror:* Bitter herbs. Generally, people eat horseradish to fulfill this ritual requirement; they may add red beet juice to mitigate the strong bitterness. A specific blessing is recited. Some dip the horseradish in ḥaroset (a mixture of nuts, fruit, and wine—and sometimes dates or other ingredients, depending on the community's tradition) to soften the taste even more. Among Sephardic Jews and Israelis (and those influenced by their tradition), bitter lettuce such as romaine frequently is used instead of horseradish.

*Korekh:* Participants in the seder eat a sandwich of sorts made of horseradish and matzah, using the bottom piece of the three ceremonial matzot. This is called "the Hillel sandwich" and usually includes ḥaroset.

*Shulḥan Orekh:* This refers to the "real" meal. Literally it means a "prepared table." The meal usually begins with a hard-boiled egg dipped in salt water. The egg is symbolic of the birth and renewal of spring. Our optimism in spring is tempered only slightly by reality in the tears of our ancestors, which are symbolized by the salt water.

*Tzafun:* This means "hidden." While there are different customs surrounding the hunt for the hidden *afikoman*, this special piece of matzah is eaten as dessert (the possible meaning of the word *afikoman*), after it is found.

*Barekh:* Blessing. Taking the form of grace after the meal (referred to in Hebrew as *Birkat ha-Mazon*), this blessing is recited over the third cup of wine.

*Hallel:* A word meaning "praise." The Hallel psalms (a specific collection from the Book of Psalms) are read and participants drink a fourth cup of wine, over which they recite the blessing. While some families may have already filled Elijah's cup with wine, many others wait to do so until this time and then symbolically open the door for him. Elijah is to announce the coming of the Messiah. Jews in the Middle Ages inserted a text of malediction at this point against those who attempt to destroy the Jewish people in reaction to the violent persecution of the Jewish people that began with the Crusades. Some scholars suggest that seder participants opened their doors at this time to undermine the blood libel accusation. However, many Jews today have opted to exclude this section from the seder.

*Nirtzah:* Accepted. The seder concludes on a messianic note: next year in Jerusalem. The singing continues, and on the second night of Passover we begin the counting of the Omer (*sefirat ha-Omer*), the period of time between Passover and Shavuot.

Some contemporary authorities argue for the addition of a fourth matzah of hope for the oppressed communities (that began with the struggle to free Soviet Jewry) and a fifth cup of wine that represents the hope potentially fulfilled in the founding of the modern state of Israel. It should also be noted that other symbols and ritual objects have found their way onto the contemporary seder table. For example, many families have placed a Miriam's Cup on the table to recognize the contribution of women to the Passover experience. This cup is filled with water as a symbol of life. ✦

# For Further Reading

### Background

Philip Goodman, *The Passover Anthology*. Philadelphia: The Jewish Publication Society of America, 1961.

Irving Greenberg, *The Jewish Way: Living the Holidays*. New York: Touchstone Books, 1988.

### Celebration and Observance

Ronald Isaacs, *Every Person's Guide to Passover*. Northvale, N.J.: Jason Aronson, 1999.

Ben Kamin, *Thinking Passover: A Rabbi's Book of Holiday Values*. New York: Dutton, 1997.

Kerry M. Olitzky, *Anticipating Revelation—Counting Our Way Through the Desert: An Omer Calendar of the Spirit*. New York: Synagogue 2000, 1998.

Michael Strassfeld, *The Jewish Holidays: A Guide and Commentary*. New York: Harper Collins Publishers, Inc. 1993.

Arthur I. Waskow, *Seasons of Our Joy: A Handbook of Jewish Festivals*. New York: Summit Books, 1986.

Ron Wolfson, *The Art of Jewish Living: The Passover Seder*. Woodstock, Vt: Jewish Lights Publishing, 1996.

### Haggadot

Joy Leavitt and Michael Strassfeld, *A Night of Questions*. Philadelphia: Reconstructionist Press, 2000.

Rachel Musleah, *Why on This Night: A Passover Haggadah for Family Celebration*. New York: Aladdin Paperbacks/Simon & Schuster, 2000.

Kerry M. Olitzky and Ronald H. Isaacs, *The Discovery Haggadah*. Hoboken, N.J.: KTAV Publishing House, 1992.

Shoshana Silberman, *In Every Generation: A Family Haggadah*. Rockville, Md.: Kar-Ben Copies, 1987.

Saul Touster, ed., *A Survivors' Haggadah*. Philadelphia: The Jewish Publication Society, 2000.

Noam Zion and David Dishon, *A Different Night*. Jerusalem: The Shalom Hartman Institute, 1997.

# Notes

## Preface

1. Debbie Friedman, music, and Debbie Friedman and Tamara Ruth Cohen, lyrics, "The Journey Song" (Sounds Write Productions, Inc. (ASCAP), 1995).

2. Numbers Rabbah 3:6.

3. Quoted in Sidney Greenberg and Pamela Roth, eds., *In Every Generation* (Northvale, N.J.: Jason Aronson, 1998), 84.

4. Quoted in Arthur Green, *The Language of Truth: The Torah Commentary of the Sefat Emet* (Philadelphia: The Jewish Publication Society, 1998), 393.

5. Irving Greenberg, *The Jewish Way: Living the Holidays* (New York: Touchstone, 1998), 53.

6. Green, *The Language of Truth*, 392.

7. Quoted in Pesach Jaffe, trans. and adapt., *Celebration of the Soul: The Holidays in the Life and Thought of Rabbi Avraham Yitzchak Kook* (Jerusalem: Genesis Press, 1992), 142.

8. Babylonian Talmud, *Pesaḥim* 6a.

9. Richard Levy, *On Wings of Freedom* (Hoboken, N.J.: KTAV Publishing Co., 1989), 10.

10. Quoted in Michael Strassfeld, *The Jewish Holidays: A Guide and Commentary* (New York: HarperCollins Publishers, Inc., 1993), 44.

## Chapter One

1. Tamara Green, "A Journey into Healing," *The Outstretched Arm* 5, no. 1 (1995), 1.

2. As retold by Rabbi Yitz Greenberg in Greenberg, *The Jewish Way*, 43.

## Chapter Two

1. Levy, *On Wings of Freedom*, 6.

*Chapter Four*

1. Babylonian Talmud, *Berakhot* 60b.

*Chapter Six*

1. "Sabbath Week," *The New York Jewish Week*, 28 May 1999.

2. Quoted in Jaffe, *Celebration of the Soul*, 136.

3. Reuven P. Bulka, *The Haggadah for Pesaḥ* (Jerusalem: Machon Pri Ha'aretz, 1985), 22.

4. Levy, *On Wings of Freedom*, 17.

*Chapter Eight*

1. As quoted in Green, *The Language of Truth*, 392.

2. The Malbim Massah: Midrash (Jerusalem: Feldheim Publishers, 1993), 4.

*Chapter Eighteen*

1. Levy, *On Wings of Freedom*, 66.

*Chapter Nineteen*

1. Lawrence A. Hoffman, *The Land of Israel: Jewish Perspectives* (South Bend, Ind.: Notre Dame, 1986), Introduction.

*Chapter Twenty*

1. Baylonian Talmud, *Nedarim* 41a.

2. *Likutei Moharan* I, 56:8–9.

*Chapter Twenty-Four*

1. Ira Stone, *Seeking the Path to Life: Theological Meditations on God and the Nature of People: Love, Life, and Death* (Woodstock, Vt.: Jewish Lights, 1992), 6.

*Chapter Thirty*

1. Jaffe, *Celebration of the Soul*, 156.

2. Stone, *Seeking the Path to Life*, 51.

## Chapter Thirty-One

1. *Orot*, 44.

2. Greenberg, *The Jewish Way*, 86.